T0282767

A Graphic Guide to Music Therapy

A Graphic Guide to Music Therapy

Bill Matney, Becca Kurtz and Mandy Griffin
Illustrated by Amy Eli Huxtable

Jessica Kingsley Publishers
London and Philadelphia

First published in Great Britain in 2024 by Jessica Kingsley Publishers
An imprint of John Murray Press

1

A CIP catalogue record for this title is available from
the British Library and the Library of Congress

ISBN 978 1 83997 728 2
eISBN 978 1 83997 729 9

Printed and bound in the United States by Integrated Books International

Jessica Kingsley Publishers' policy is to use papers that are natural,
renewable and recyclable products and made from wood grown in
sustainable forests. The logging and manufacturing processes are expected
to conform to the environmental regulations of the country of origin.

Jessica Kingsley Publishers
Carmelite House
50 Victoria Embankment
London EC4Y 0DZ

www.jkp.com

John Murray Press
Part of Hodder & Stoughton Ltd
An Hachette Company

Table of Contents

Acknowledgments

All: We would like to thank the many authors of other publications and videos who have helped us to introduce and highlight the field and profession of music therapy.

We would also like to thank Jessica Kingsley Publishers, for initiating this project, and for their guidance along the way.

Bill: I would first and foremost like to share my appreciation for my co-authors/collaborators on this exciting and unique project. I've had opportunities to work with art therapists as a clinician. So, when the opportunity to work with music therapists and an art therapist on a book arose, I jumped at the chance. To see these words come to life through visual artwork, especially in a way so accessible to everyone, has in itself made this project worthwhile to me. So, I offer my sincere gratitude to Amy Eli Huxtable.

I would also like to thank my academic colleagues and students at the University of Kansas, as well as those clinicians, music therapy educators, and students I know from across the world; they have shared their knowledge and experiences in ways that have certainly influenced the perspectives I have contributed to this book.

Lastly, I would like to offer gratitude for my family, who have been supportive of my endeavors as a clinician, researcher, and teacher. And with this in mind, I would like to dedicate my contributions to this book to my mother, Carolyn Matney, who continues to live through the music I share with others.

Amy: Thank you to Bill, Mandy, and Becca for all their knowledge, creativity, and dedication that went into this project. It has been a pleasure to learn more about music therapy from these passionate professionals.

I would also like to thank Libby Schmanke and Gaelynn Wolf Bordonaro for igniting my illustrating spark. To the expressive therapy team at Marillac, thank you for your support along the way. I'd also like to thank my spouse, Grahm Mahanna, for always cheering me on.

Mandy: I am very grateful for my co-authors and am so pleased that we have been able to work on this informative and fun project together. The idea of a graphic guide for expressive arts is amazing, and Amy, you are an illustrating and concept wizard! Thank you for pioneering the way and also bringing to life our words on music therapy.

I also wouldn't be the clinician I am today without my mentors during my time at the University of Kansas, as well as those recreational, music, and art therapists I've worked with. To all the folks I've worked with in mental health specializing in other disciplines, I have been so lucky to have so much knowledge shared with me that has helped me grow as a music therapist and person. I am blessed to get to work with all the individuals I do, including those I serve with and those we serve—so, thank you all!

Finally, I would like to thank my family, whose support across the years has been a shining light throughout my life. I would also like to dedicate my contributions in this book to my mother, Julie Helms, who was always my biggest supporter and would have handed everyone she met a copy of this book.

Becca: I am just so grateful for the fellow members of the "Graphic Guide Club," as they have been incredibly supportive throughout the major life events I've experienced over the course of this project. Their passion for their various areas of expertise gives me life! I have grown so much through our discussions, and they have challenged me to expand beyond the rigidity that often comes with years of formal academic writing. I admire the confidence and experience with writing, illustrating, and publishing that they bring to the table!

I also extend my immense gratitude to my creative arts therapy colleagues and mentors with whom I have had the joy of working throughout my career: my professors and classmates at the University of Kansas who helped me build a solid foundation in my music therapy knowledge, and clinical skills; the expressive therapy team at the University of Kansas Health System Marillac Campus, who helped me understand the value of interprofessional collaboration, and experience the beauty of art therapy, recreation therapy, and drama therapy; and my music therapy colleagues at the University of Iowa Health Care, who helped me discover my passion for the medical setting as an intern, and who continue to help me grow as a clinician every day as co-workers.

Finally, I would like to thank my family, especially my partner, Brian, for their consistent encouragement throughout this process. I also would like to thank two women who are near and dear to my heart: my mother, a nurse of 41 years, for inspiring me to pursue a career in healthcare; and my grandmother, a lifelong musician and teacher, for encouraging me to engage with music throughout my life. From my first piano recital to my senior carillon and voice recitals, both of your support means so much.

Preface

I wonder how many of you expected the illustrator to write some of the preface; I do like to be unpredictable. Here's hoping I can start you off on a good note.

I wrote and illustrated *A Graphic Guide to Art Therapy*, with the help of my professors, Libby Schmanke and Gaelynn Wolf Bordonaro. The graphic novel style lent itself well to those interested in learning about art therapy. In the fall of 2021, Jessica Kingsley Publishers reached out to me, suggesting that this format would also work well for music therapy. I couldn't agree more.

As you may have gathered, I am not a music therapist. I was in no way qualified to write this book. So, cue the 1980's montage where the team for *A Graphic Guide to Music Therapy* comes together. I'm cruising along in my red convertible, picking up people along the way, maybe with some New Wave music playing in the background.

At the time, I worked with Becca Kurtz on the same expressive therapy team. I asked if she would be interested in co-writing a graphic novel, and she opened the car door and hopped right in. Meanwhile, I told a fellow art therapist that we were starting this project, to which she responded, "I work with a music therapist who has a background in creative writing!" That's when we parked the car and picked up Mandy Griffin.

Becca, Mandy, and I brainstormed ideas for a third author for about two seconds before both of them said, "Bill Matney!" When we contacted Bill, he was eager to join our journey. We drove his way to pick him up, and once we were at his location, Bill put his driving cap on and took the wheel.

Bill, you've been our driver for the bulk of this project. We're down to our last mile on the highway. How about taking the controls one last time and finishing this preface?

—*Amy Eli Huxtable*

Imagine looking out of your window and seeing this dream team in a red convertible while Tears for Fears blares in the background! The invitation to collaborate interprofessionally on a graphic book about music therapy also took me about two seconds to commit to. I was excited to get to know Amy, and to get to work with the group. The road trip began!

Reading Amy's book, *A Graphic Guide to Art Therapy*, gave us wonderful ideas and a helpful structure to start with; we all also saw new directions that would fit both our backgrounds and the field of music therapy. Watching our text on concepts, history, methods, populations (and more) come to life through visuals was constantly inspiring to the three of us, who often live in worlds of sound. I appreciated the ability for each of us to offer and discuss visual ideas, but also to just give space for Amy to make the magic happen.

At the outset, we felt as if this book should introduce what music therapy is, with a focus on the power of simplicity and breadth; we wanted anyone who was curious to be able to pick up the book and feel comfortable with it, regardless of whether they had any idea what music therapy is or not. We could see this book being used supplementally in an introductory course at a university, or in a broader music and health course. We also think there are ideas we share that aren't always covered in a standard introduction to music therapy book...these ideas may be a little unique or rarely discussed in the field, in part because some of them are relatively new.

So, who are we? We are three music therapists putting our experience and knowledge down in words, in different areas of interest and experience, in ways that we hope are straightforward but interesting. We also have an art therapist who took the time and thought to convert those words to artistic visuals. But, what we found out is that each of us contributed to the music, art, and therapy being presented.

It's been an amazing group road trip, and I can't wait for people to see the pictures!

Sincerely, the Graphic Guide Club (1980's music amplifies and then slowly fades as credits scroll...)

—*Bill Matney*

Introduction
Hello! It's nice to meet you!

I'm guessing you are here because you are interested in or curious about music therapy.

It's a fascinating topic and a really interesting professional field!

Perhaps you picked up this book because...

You are studying music therapy as an undergraduate or graduate student?

You are thinking about studying music therapy in the future?

You are a music therapist who likes books?

You know music therapists or a little about music therapy but want to know more about it?

You know that a book with pictures, music, and video is going to be fun?

Any combination of the above?

Well, it's wonderful you are here!

Introducing Music Therapy

So, what is music therapy? Instead of starting with a definition (which we will get to later), let's describe music therapy based on some straightforward ideas.

Let's explore these ideas by considering how things that happen in our everyday lives, including music,[1] can help us be healthier.

Everyday Life

In our everyday lives, we move, communicate, work, play, and engage with many things throughout the day.

Music is something we engage with, sometimes with intention and focus.

But sometimes music is just in the environments we work and play in, happening around us.

Everyday Life Example: Movement

Movement is a part of our everyday lives. We may exercise and play sports to help promote our physical health. These activities may be therapeutic in a general sense, and can definitely be important!

We may employ a personal trainer (who is specialized) to help maximize or focus our intention to improve physically and be healthier. The trainer's knowledge and expertise can facilitate better results for us.

In certain circumstances, especially when our movement is compromised, we may also see a qualified professional, a physical therapist, to address very specific health-related needs.

Everyday Life Example: Communication

Communication is a part of our everyday lives. We speak to people in many environments for different purposes.

Sometimes, when stressed, we communicate with a friend to let off steam. This communication and verbal processing can be therapeutic in a general sense.

We might also communicate with a mentor, such as a teacher, to focus on particular areas of need. This communication may help us think through things more clearly and make informed decisions.

When our thoughts or communication seem off, or when we proactively want to focus on communication and thinking to benefit our health, we can work with a counselor or psychologist to help us address specific needs.

Everyday Life and Music

OK, we are returning to music now! Yay!

In our everyday lives, music may be all around us, including at the store, in a television show or movie, or on our phones.

We may choose to engage with music directly, such as by actively listening, singing, playing instruments, or dancing. These engaging experiences may energize us, help us relax, or give us an "escape" from daily tasks.

Everyday Life and Music

That's right. I am a champion.

We may also use music to help us move and exercise, such as when we take a run or do a work out. The music might even help us pace our movements and help us to feel motivated.

♫♪ ...H, I, J, K, elemeno P, Q... ♪♫

We may use music to help us organize and learn something, like when we sing the alphabet song as children to learn the letters. The music can give us a particular way to focus, attend, remember, and sequence things.

We may use music to help us emote and express ourselves in unique ways, whether actively listening, singing, or playing an instrument.

Everyday Life and Music

In these ways and others, we might say that our own uses of music can be individually beneficial, or even therapeutic, for us.

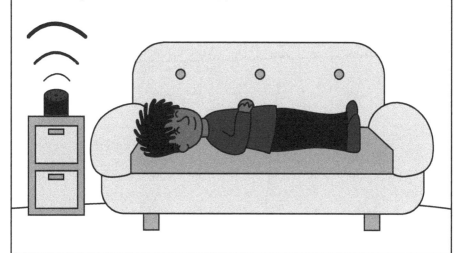

In a similar way that a physical therapist or counselor uses their respective expertise with movement or verbal processing, a music therapist specializes in implementing music in ways that can uniquely address a range of health and well-being needs.

Talking About Music

Many artists have mentioned how talking or writing about music is limiting, that it's like "dancing about architecture."[2]

This is my dance about the Eiffel Tower!

Defining music or music therapy through words can be helpful, but is probably not enough to completely communicate what it is and how it works. That being said, we can allow definitions and descriptions to help inform us and still be open to music therapy being "more than words."

What is Music?

Music is often described as sound happening through time, typically in some organized way that people find some kind of value in.

We often use a set of characteristics that help organize music and give it shape, including, but not limited to, timbre, pitch, rhythmic qualities, tempo, melody, harmony, form, and style/genre. We will discuss these characteristics in more detail later.

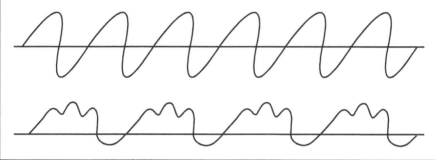

You still in there?

Yes! You mentioned high school, which made me think of a song that played at prom... Now it's stuck in my head!

Because sound is created through physical vibrations, it is often heard. But, one can access/experience music without hearing it; music is also tactile, visual, and can be engaged with through memory as well.

Music is always culturally situated. While we can find ways that different types of music connect to each other, they are also each uniquely and contextually valuable.

A Conceptual Definition of Music Therapy

The field of music therapy can be understood as the intentional use, by a qualified music therapist, of music, music involvement, and the relationship that develops through shared experiences, to promote health in physiological, cognitive, communicative, social, emotional, and spiritual domains.[3]

Some Professional Definitions of Music Therapy

Professional definitions provide us with an understanding of how the profession views the work that music therapists do. There are overlaps between the conceptual and professional definitions, but different areas of focus. Here are three examples of professional definitions.

In the United States, the common professional definition of music therapy is provided by the American Music Therapy Association: "The clinical and evidence-based use of music interventions to accomplish individualized goals within a therapeutic relationship by a credentialed professional who has completed an approved music therapy program."

The British Association for Music Therapy defines music therapy as: "An established psychological clinical intervention, delivered by HCPC [Health and Care Professions Council]-registered music therapists to help people whose lives have been affected by injury, illness or disability through supporting their psychological, emotional, cognitive, physical, communicative and social needs."

The Australian Music Therapy Association defines music therapy as: "A research-based allied health profession in which music is used to actively support people as they aim to improve their health, functioning and well-being. It can help people of all ages to manage their physical and mental health and enhance their quality of life."

What Does it Mean to be Trained and Qualified?

Music therapists in the United States have completed a minimum of a bachelor's level degree at an American Music Therapy Association (AMTA)-approved college or university program and have also completed 1200 hours of clinical training, including a supervised internship. After completing an internship, music therapists are eligible to sit for the national board certification exam. On passing this exam, music therapists obtain the title MT-BC,[4] which is required to practice professionally in many settings in the United States. Every five years, music therapists must have completed 100 hours of continuing education to be eligible for re-certification, which ensures that music therapists continue to develop their knowledge and clinical skills.[5]

Music therapists in the UK have completed a master's level degree in music therapy and must be registered with the Health and Care Professions Council to practice in the field. Registered music therapists must also take continuing professional development courses to maintain their knowledge and learn of new developments in the field of music therapy.[6]

Music therapists in Australia have completed an Australian Music Therapy Association-approved training at master's degree level. On completion of the program, music therapists must apply for registration with the Australian Music Therapy Association in order to be eligible for practice. They must take continuing education to maintain their skills.[7]

Wow! That's a lot of training!

Definitely! We need to be sure we can provide quality care for our clients.

What Does "Evidence-Based" Mean?

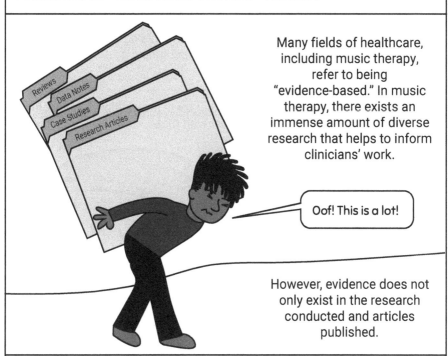

Many fields of healthcare, including music therapy, refer to being "evidence-based." In music therapy, there exists an immense amount of diverse research that helps to inform clinicians' work.

Oof! This is a lot!

However, evidence does not only exist in the research conducted and articles published.

We as clinicians acknowledge that our own professional experiences, as well as the prior and immediate experiences of clients that we work with, are also contributing to the larger body of "evidence" that informs how we work in the moment.

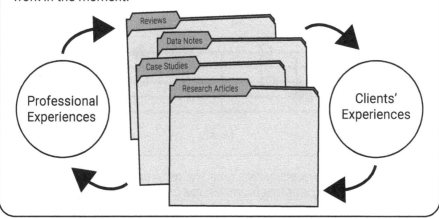

What Does "Relationship" Mean?

As in many healthcare professions, a music therapist develops a relationship with their clients, which includes building rapport and trust. The depth of this relationship will differ according to the setting and context.

The below visual helps us understand that there are multiple relationships going on: therapist with client, therapist with music, and client with music.

The ways that these relationships exist and grow depend on many factors, including the setting, approach, and client's prior experiences.

What are Some Goals in Music Therapy?

What are Some Goals in Music Therapy?

Promote the use of language and improve speech/articulation

Improve or maintain cognitive skills, such as attention, memory, and identification of numbers, letters, colors, and other items

One way to do this is by writing a song with a melody that helps us remember something.

These are only examples of some general goals that may be addressed in music therapy sessions. We will look at more specific examples later in the book.

What Instruments are Used in Music Therapy?

Music therapists most commonly use their voices, guitar, piano, world percussion instruments, auxiliary percussion instruments, Orff percussion instruments, body percussion, and music technology in their work.[8]

They may use other accompaniment instruments as well, such as ukelele and autoharp. They also use recordings of songs for particular types of experiences.

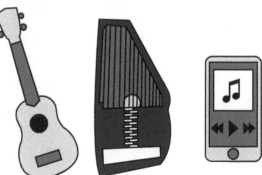

What Types of Music are Used in Music Therapy?

Music therapists are trained in musicianship through many styles of music, including classical music. More relevant to our work is our musicianship in popular, folk, diverse global music, and a broad range of genres (such as country, rock, soul, hip hop, and more!).

What Types of Music are Used in Music Therapy?

Music therapy musicianship is unique because it is always in relationship with the clients/participants; music therapists choose which methods work best in the context of the session. They are also capable of modifying music within these methods, largely through the characteristics of music. We will discuss these characteristics in more detail later!

When someone mentions music therapy, sometimes people have different ideas and misconceptions about what it is. Let's talk about

Some Common Misunderstandings About Music Therapy.

Some Common Misunderstandings

Common Misunderstanding Alert: "Clients/Participants must have prior experience with music to be involved."

Part of a music therapist's job is to make music experiences accessible to every person regardless of experience.

Black keys make up a type of scale that sounds good no matter which note you play!

Some Common Misunderstandings

Common Misunderstanding Alert:
"Any musician is a music therapist."

While musicians can perform powerful music that people may connect with in beneficial ways, music therapists are unique musicians who are less focused on performance; they are trained professionals who use their years of knowledge of psychology, anatomy, music neuroscience, human development, research of various types, and shared music making to facilitate therapeutic music experiences.

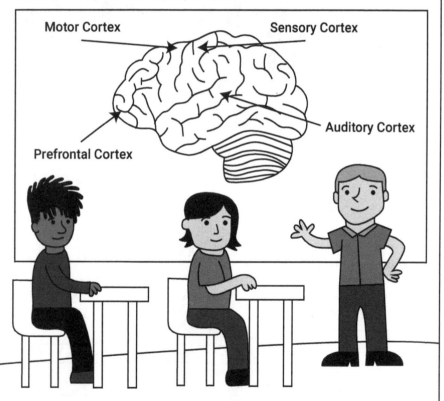

Music therapy education includes a variety of topics, like neuroscience...

Music and Health: Some Histories

The idea that music is related to health is long standing; it is at least as old as the documented cultural histories we have located.

Ancient Greek writers talked about how the universe is musical,[1] as well as how music can interact with...

...our bodies,

our character development,

and our communal growth.[2]

Music and Health: Some Histories

Even before the Greek writers, Egyptian medical papyri suggested that music had an influence on the human body all the way back to 1500 BCE.[3] The use of song and chant by music healers and priests was common in ritual and was believed to thwart evil that manifested in disease.

Music and Health: Some Histories

Of course, Ancient Greece and Egypt are only two histories among many histories of music and health. For example, we can look at ideas and languages in Nigeria and surrounding areas.

The word Egwu, of the Igbo people, refers to drum, drumming, dance, music, sport, and health.[4] Similarly, the word Ngoma, of the Bantuic people, refers to drums, drumming, music, and healing.[5]

Music and Health: Some Histories

In China, music and medicine have historically been connected.

We can even see the words in written form are very similar, and originate from the same oracle bone script.[6]

The character on the left is for music, and the one on the right is for medicine.

Wow! Those **are** super similar!

Music   Medicine

Music and Health: Some Histories

Ancient Vedic literature has also suggested the importance of music and the science behind it to promote health through specific intonations, rhythmic forms, harmonic modes, and melodies.[7]

The Beginning of Music Therapy as a Profession

Traction for music therapy as a professional field occurred in the United States beginning in the later 1800s but more particularly during and between World Wars I and II.

Eva Vescelius, Margaret Anderton, Isa Maud Ilsen, and Harriet Seymour were a few of the many important figures who contributed to music and health practice through advocacy, presentations, practical work, and training prior to the professional field being developed.[8]

The Beginning of Music Therapy as a Profession

The modern professional field of music therapy originated right after World War II. Musicians were providing music experiences in hospitals for soldiers who were returning from the war.

The results they were seeing prompted an increase in discussion about how people could be trained and qualified to provide music therapy services. Universities began offering courses, and later established degree programs.[9]

Professional Organizations

Two professional organizations were originally created in the United States: the National Association for Music Therapy and the American Association for Music Therapy. These two associations merged to form the American Music Therapy Association in 1998.

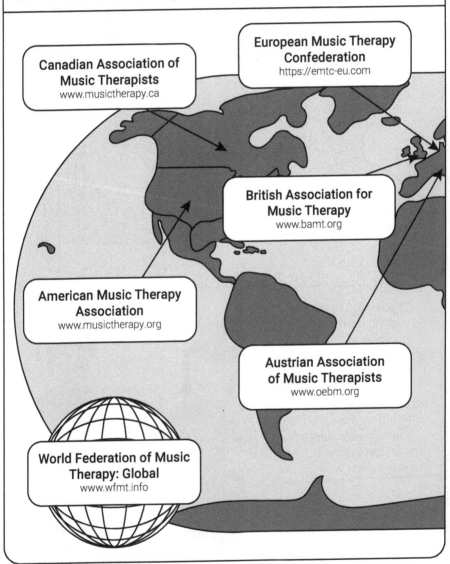

Canadian Association of
Music Therapists
www.musictherapy.ca

European Music Therapy
Confederation
https://emtc-eu.com

British Association for
Music Therapy
www.bamt.org

American Music Therapy
Association
www.musictherapy.org

Austrian Association
of Music Therapists
www.oebm.org

World Federation of Music
Therapy: Global
www.wfmt.info

Professional Organizations

Many other countries also developed national organizations that support practice in their respective countries. There is even a World Federation of Music Therapy.

Swedish Association for Music Therapists
www.musikterapeut.se

Finnish Society for Music Therapy
www.musiikkiterapia.fi

Japanese Music Therapy Association
www.jmta.jp/en

Music Therapy Association of the Czech Republic
www.czmta.cz

Chinese Music Therapist Association
www.chinamusictherapy.org

Music Therapy Association of Taiwan
www.musictherapy.com.tw

Hong Kong Music Therapy Association
www.musictherapyhk.org

Australian Music Therapy Association
www.austmta.org.au

Board Certification

The Certification Board for Music Therapists acts as the accrediting entity for music therapists, primarily in the United States but also around the world. You will see music therapists put the initials MT-BC after their name, meaning they are a board-certified music therapist. That means they have completed coursework within a degree, completed an internship, passed a board-certification examination, and fulfilled continuing education requirements.

State Recognition and Licensure

More recently, some states in the United States have adopted legislation so that music therapists are specifically recognized as healthcare professionals, while others have adopted legislation where music therapists have to be licensed to practice. These legal measures help people gain access to services and protect people from those who are not trained.

Music therapy licensure as of now focuses on being board certified through the Certification Board for Music Therapists.

Each state may then have slightly different stipulations, but are overall pretty consistent with requirements.

Summary

So, we've described music therapy and talked about the role of a music therapist. We've also briefly talked about the history of music and health in different cultures, up to the beginning of music therapy as a profession.

But we haven't got too much into what music therapy looks and sounds like, or how it operates and functions. Let's head that direction now!

WALK THIS WAY

Functions

Earlier we talked about some ways that we relate to music and use music in our everyday lives. We can talk about how music can function in relation to health along the same lines.[1] Some of the more common ways music connects to our health are listed below.

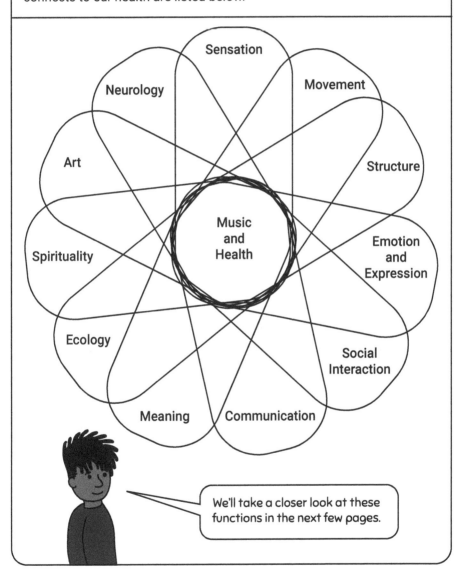

We'll take a closer look at these functions in the next few pages.

Sensation

First, music engages the senses. We hear, feel, and see music when we listen to it and play it.

Movement

Music can promote and influence movement, including moving in structured ways.

Because music is sound happening through time, listening to music can promote organized movement, such as walking.

Instrument play uses many different types of movement with fingers, hands, arms, and other parts of the body.

Organization and Structure

Music can organize and give structure to other things as well, including learning, memory, and events.

♫♪ ...Japan, Indonesia, Turkey, Thailand, Nepal, Sri Lanka, China... ♪♫

We can use music to remember something (like the alphabet, or states in a country, or sequencing a task).

We can also use the structure of music to help organize an act, an event, or a ceremony.

Emotion and Expression

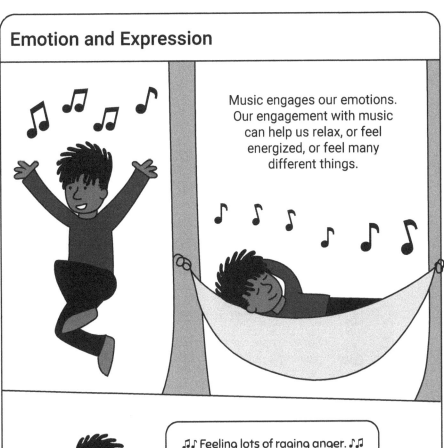

Music engages our emotions. Our engagement with music can help us relax, or feel energized, or feel many different things.

♫♪ Feeling lots of raging anger. ♫♪
♫♪ Turning it into a banger. ♫♪

So, active music making can be a unique form of individual expression that can be tied to our emotional states.

Communication and Language

Music is often talked about as its own unique type of communication.

Music and verbal language share many characteristics, particularly in regard to rhythm, pitch, and timbre.[2] When we speak, we can use these qualities to enhance meaning.

> Did you put this whoopee cushion on my chair?

> Who, **me**? I would **never** do something like that!

For example, we change pitches when asking a question or using sarcasm.

In some cases, characteristics of music from a particular culture can even be linked to specific characteristics of languages of that same culture.[3]

> English is a stress-timed language, while Spanish is a syllable-timed language. Do you see the similarities in rhythm between language and music?

     ×   ×
The **tea**cher is **in**terested
     ×   ×
in **buy**ing some **books**.

♫♪ The **rain** in **Spain** falls
  ×   ×
mainly in the **plain**. ♪♫

          ×
A los **ni**ños les gustan
los perros.

♫♪ ...mi burrito saba**ne**ro,
             ×
voy camino de be**lén**... ♪♫

Music and Health: Meaning

Music can reflect and promote individual or shared meaning. These meanings may be related to the first time we heard a particular song, or may be spontaneous and create new meaning in the moment.

Social Interaction

Music can be shared; it offers a distinct way to interact (and even communicate) with others.

Sociocultural Connections

Music can be connected to our individual and shared histories.

We often associate music experiences in our past to particular events, places, and people.

Oh my gosh, I love this song! It takes me back to high school. My friends and I would drive around and sing this at the top of our lungs!

Really? This song reminds me of a break-up. It was playing in the background when my partner dumped me at the Pizza Shack.

Music can also (like all other arts) exemplify aspects of the cultures we belong to.

♪♪ ...coquí, coquí, coquí, qui, qui, qui... ♪♪

Ecology

Music has a dynamic relationship with environments, communities, and cultures.

Traditional musical instruments originated through materials available in a particular area.

Qualities of different music also arise through the interactions between those instruments and the ideas that people in those areas have.

Spirituality

Music can be a part of our lives in ways that connect us to something larger than ourselves, whether we personally view that as connecting to a higher power, to the universe, to ancestors, to each other, or to something else.

We see the importance of music in religious and spiritual writings and events all over the world.

Art

Music can be pleasing, beautiful, and creative.

Music can give us an alternate
way of being in or with the world.

The Brain

Research also shows that music is uniquely situated in the brain; it can activate neurological centers and new brain pathways in many domains of health (including, but not limited to, sensation, movement, emotion, and communication/language).[4]

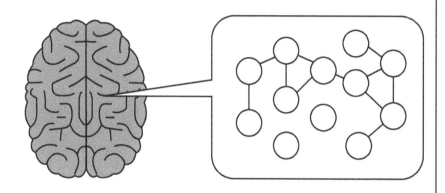

In this sense, music can act as a flexible "technology" that promotes brain engagement and new neural pathways for growth.

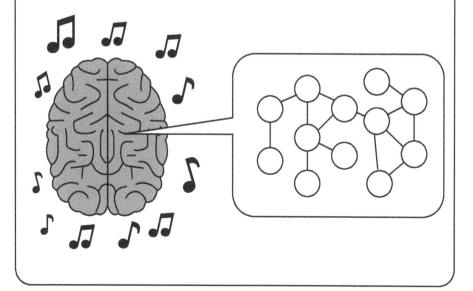

Summary

We now have a better understanding of many of the ways music connects to health in general.

So, let's go ahead and look at some music therapy methods!

Sensation

Neurology

Movement

Art

Structure

Music and Health

Spirituality

Emotion and Expression

Ecology

Social Interaction

Meaning

Communication

There are a few different

Music Therapy Methods

and ways to engage with music.
Let's take a look at these!

The Four Music Therapy Methods[1]

We commonly experience music in four different but connected ways.

♫♪ He rocks in the tree tops all day long. Hoppin' and a–boppin' and a–singin' his song. ♫♫

We **re-create** music when we play music that already exists. Singing/playing a popular song is a type of re-creating.

We **compose** music when we create music that did not exist before. We can compose on an instrument or by using music notation. Others might re-create our composition later.

The Four Music Therapy Methods

We **improvise** music when we create something new in the musical moment that won't ever really be re-created in the same way. Jazz often uses improvisation, as do many other styles of music.

We **receive** music, usually by listening to it. But we can also sense music in other ways, such as feeling the vibrations that loud speakers give off.

While each of these experiences is connected to the others, there is usually one that is primary. When music therapists facilitate music engagement using these types of experiences, we call them music therapy methods.

Ways to Engage with Music

Within the four music therapy methods, there are many ways music engagement can occur. Three ways that we engage with music in a more active sense include the following:

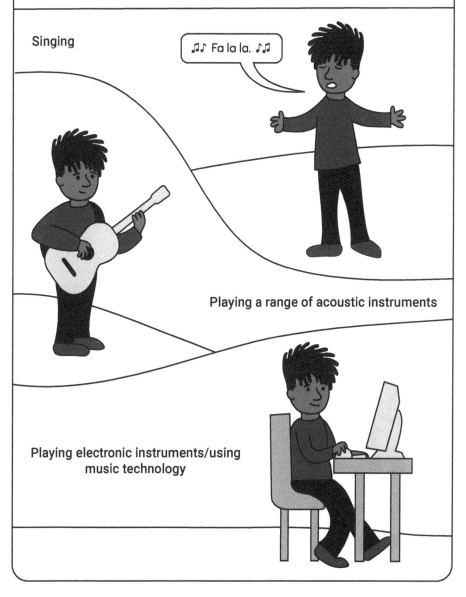

Singing

Playing a range of acoustic instruments

Playing electronic instruments/using music technology

Ways to Engage in Music Therapy

Music therapists work with people individually, in groups, with families, and with communities, through the four music therapy methods, using voices, other instruments, and recorded music. We can already see that there is a lot of variety in how music therapy can look!

Music Therapy with Individuals

Music Therapy Groups

Ways to Engage in Music Therapy

Music Therapy with Families

Music Therapy with Communities

♪♪ We shall not be moved. ♪♪

Summary

Later in the book we will discuss these four methods and some of the more specific, common ways they are used in music therapy processes and interventions. We will call these more specific uses therapeutic music experiences.

Characteristics of Music

The characteristics of music include those items that play a role in the organizing of the sounds we sense. These characteristics can't ever really be separated entirely from each other. But some may be emphasized more than others for particular reasons. Let's discuss each of these characteristics.

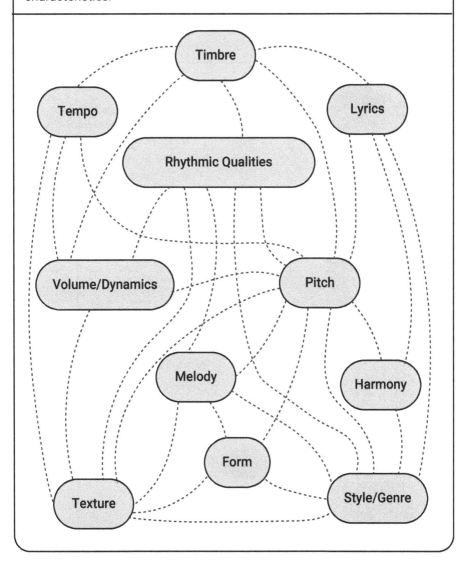

Tempo

Tempo refers to the speed at which the music is occurring. As you can imagine, faster tempos tend to be more energizing to us, while slower tempos tend to be more relaxing.

For example, we use tempo as a part of music to help people to move/exercise at a particular speed, to remember or say words at a particular speed, to relax, to lower or raise their heart rate and/or breathing rate, and many other reasons!

Rhythmic Qualities

Rhythm largely means how sound is organized over time, outside its tempo. Some music has simple, consistent, and predictable rhythms while other music has more complex, syncopated, and even changing rhythms (such as the be bop era of jazz). Specific rhythms are also a very important part of different styles of music.

Music therapists consider qualities of rhythm when choosing recorded music, when composing, when supporting clients improvising on instruments, when re-creating songs, and when facilitating movement to music.

Volume

Music therapists take into account what role volume has in music experiences. Lower volumes will more likely be used for relaxing. A song used for relaxation also often has somewhat limited changes in volume over time. Someone may be expressing themselves by playing music at a higher volume, which can provide a sense of control, offer them auditory and kinesthetic feedback while they play, allow for processing of emotions expressed, and can even be relaxing.[1]

Pitch

Pitch refers to the perceived highness or lowness of the sound. Most instruments, including our voices, have some kind of pitch and pitch range, including drums, when compared to each other. We each hear in a pitch range and sing in a pitch range. So, music therapists take into account pitch ranges when working with clients.

Timbre

Timbre refers to the characteristics of sound that are not related to pitch or volume. Even two violins playing the same note can still sound a little different due to the timbre of the sound. Some instruments, such as many types of drums, rely more on timbre for their sound quality than other instruments, such as a piano. Organ sounds create many timbres!

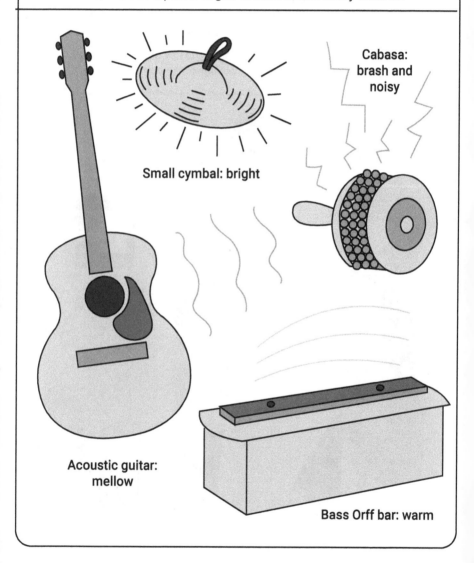

Small cymbal: bright

Cabasa: brash and noisy

Acoustic guitar: mellow

Bass Orff bar: warm

Melody

A song has a set of pitches that together make up a melody. Melodies can include pitches that are close together and move in a common way, or can jump around and be less predictable. Music therapists can take into account how a melody is put together in relation to a client's abilities and goals.

Harmony

Harmony in music is when a set of pitches happen at the same time. When you play a piano or guitar, you often play chords that provide harmonic structure to the music. Depending on the notes being played, harmonies may sound consonant (sound good together) or dissonant (create tension between notes). We become accustomed to particular patterns of harmony in songs, and can be intrigued by new patterns.

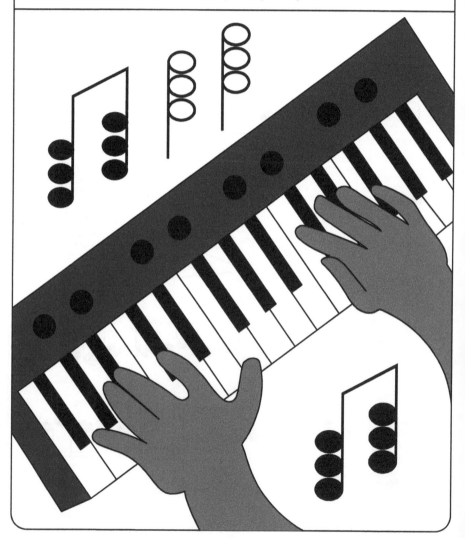

Lyrics

Lyrics are the words within songs. They add meanings that we may resonate with. They allow us to express ourselves when we write songs. They can give us a set of tasks to do. They can even be used to learn something new through music. Music therapists may use lyrics in music to do many things, such as promote movement, write a song about a topic, and analyze meaning in a topic.

Texture

Texture describes the many layers of sound that can happen in music, and when those layers are added or removed. For example, when a band is playing or choir is singing, some parts might come in or stop at different times. Texture changes levels of complexity when listening, and types of interactions when playing instruments.

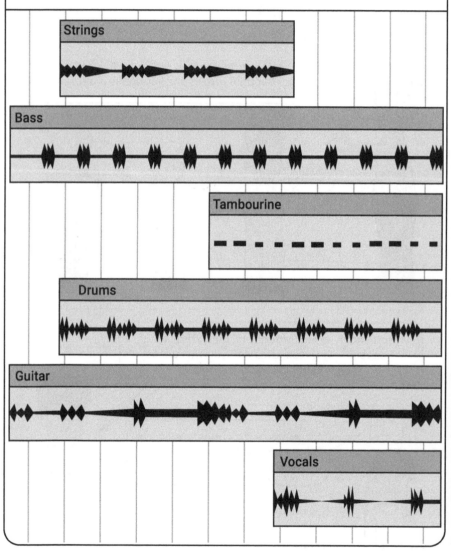

Form

Form refers to the way music is organized in a song or composition. In popular and folk music we can think of the form of the words, such as a verse and a chorus. Twelve-bar blues is a form that often uses repetition in lyrics and melodies. Music therapists can use the form of a song, and components such as repetition, to help address particular needs with clients.

Style/Genre

Music is created all over the world by people with ideas about how the characteristics of music can combine uniquely. These ideas sometimes proliferate into styles, or genres, of music. Styles of music represent cultural ideas that include the way music sounds, but also the creation of instruments themselves. Styles can also evolve over time.

Metal

Hip hop

These are just a few of the many styles of music!

Joropo

Bluegrass

The characteristics of music are only part of the picture, because music is a shared process and a shared experience. Let's chat a little about the

Qualities of Musicking.

Some Qualities of Musicking

Musicking has been described as musical events that occur through a set of relationships: sound and sound, people and sound, and people and people.[1] We can also weave into these relationships the ways we relate with the music instruments.

So, not only are music therapists thinking about the characteristics of the sound itself, but also the ways people are interacting through the sound and the instruments being played. Let's discuss some qualities of musicking!

Progressive Accessibility

Music making is sometimes thought of as a pursuit of art that requires self-discipline, or even "genius" and "perfection." While music therapists are musicians who understand the beauty of music, they also study music to help make it accessible and beautiful to people regardless of their prior background and experiences with music.

Instruments have the capacity to be made easier to play, and they also can be studied for an entire lifetime. Music therapists therefore facilitate the *progressive accessibility* of music making so that people can feel accomplished and fulfilled, and enjoy the beauty of music experiences.

To see and hear more about Orff instruments, and the pentatonic scale, you can watch this video by music therapist, Orff Schulwerk presenter, and performer Kalani Das.

www.youtube.com/watch?v=kGF5vhj_Dcc

Musicking and Flow

Flow state, a psychological theory proposed by Mihaly Csikszentmihalyi,[2] is a place where you feel focused on and optimal in your performance of a task. Music can work well with flow state because it changes over time, can be progressively accessible in terms of level of challenge, and people can develop creatively through it. Music therapists work with clients to navigate structure and safety along with creativity and challenge in order to promote an optimal place of being within music.

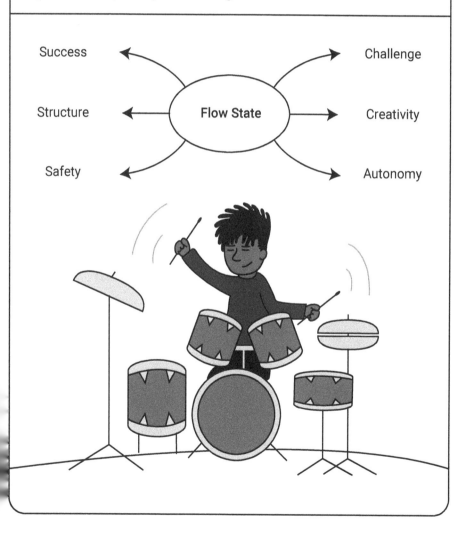

Musical Actions

The following table describes many actions that can be used to make sound on music instruments.[3] These actions might be used by themselves or in combinations, depending on the instrument being played. These techniques can help people to understand traditional techniques on instruments, but also how to be creative on them! There are some common examples below.

Action Types		Instrument Examples
Contact		
Touch		Wind chimes Music apps on phone
	Press	Piano Trumpet keys Drum machine Muting a cymbal
Tap		Frame drum Woodblock Drum machine

Musical Actions

Action Types	Instrument Examples
Strike	Djembe Piano Snare drum
Brush/Rub	Frame drum Cuica Turntable Violin
Scrape	Cabasa Guiro
Flick	Tone chimes Vibratone

Musical Actions

Action Types	Instrument Examples
Shake	Maracas
Caress	Ocean drum Hoof rattle
Rattle	Rattles Shekere

Musical Actions

Action Types	Instrument Examples
Pluck	Banjo Harp Mbira Guitar
Strum	Guitar Ukulele Harp
Move Body	Theremin Roland Handsonic Adaptive software instruments
Move Air	Voice Trumpet Recorder

Sensory Feedback of Instrumentation

When we play musical instruments, many of our senses can be engaged. For example, we feel the instruments through the actions we just discussed. But we may also feel the instrumental sound itself. For example, large drums and large speakers can vibrate enough that we actually feel the sound. Any instrument we play includes our kinesthetic (touch) experience of it, and the feedback it gives us. We can feel reinforced, stimulated, and structured through that feedback. These experiences can be taken into account, for example, with people who need more tactile input or have some sensory aversion.

Some clients need extra tactile input and like to use cabasas on their arms. Personally, I think it's too tickly!

Entrainment

Entrainment is a physical and physiological process that occurs when things and/or people synchronize in time with each other. Entrainment was originally realized when physicist Christiaan Huygens noticed how pendulum clocks would synchronize with each other over time.

Music therapists use the rhythmic qualities of music to help people synchronize their playing and their movement in real time. Studies further suggest that physiological entrainment can also promote psychosocial connections.[4]

Attunement[5]

We bring ourselves when we make music or listen to it. We can also personally align with the music we listen to, and with the people we make music with. The word attunement means to be receptive to, and to align with. Music therapists often seek to attune with the actions and musical expressions of the people they work with, or to attune a client's current state with the music that they may listen to for a particular purpose.

The Song in My Head!

Have you ever had a song or a melody stay with you for a while? Or, have you ever listened to a song that you haven't heard in years and then just started singing the words immediately? Music organizes in ways we may find beautiful, or we may hear tunes as "dins in our head." Song melodies can be catchy and stay with us, whether on "repeat" in our heads for a little while during a day, or accessed later.

Music resides in our brains in unique places, and can be accessed even when remembering other things is challenging (for example, when someone has dementia). Music therapists use this mnemonic power of music with clients in many ways.

Programmatic Intention and Meaning

Many kinds of music, even instrumental music, have already embedded within them a ritual, a story, or other kind of programmatic intention. We can think of holiday songs, songs at places of worship, and songs at sporting events, but there are also many other situations and places where we use music to enhance meaning.

Rituals and stories contain meaning that can become part of a therapeutic process. But using these in therapy requires reflection, honoring cultural ideas, and avoiding cultural appropriation. New rituals, stories, and other kinds of meaning can also be produced through music making in the moment and through repeated music experiences.

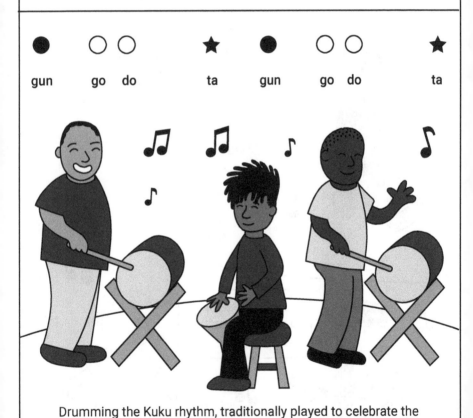

Drumming the Kuku rhythm, traditionally played to celebrate the women bringing fish back to the village for food.

A combination of

Music and Other Modalities

often makes a great team!
Let's see how they work together.

Music and More

Sometimes music therapists incorporate other modalities to supplement music experiences, including, but not limited to, what you see in the visual below.

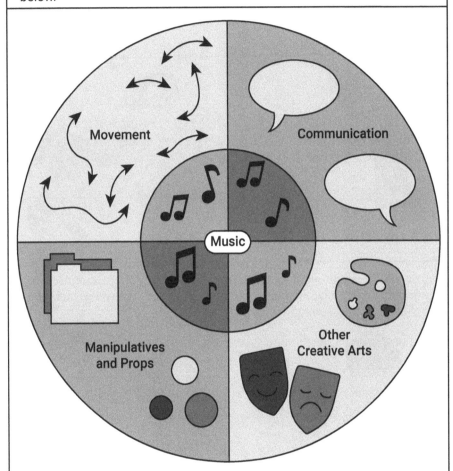

Each of these modalities is used within the scope of a music therapist's training, knowledge, and experience; they are sometimes used with consultation from or collaboration with other professionals.

Let's talk about some of these modalities.

Movement

Music is commonly associated with movement and dance, so music therapists use this connection (sometimes with movement as the intended outcome).

A music therapist might receive consultation from or collaborate with a physical therapist, occupational therapist, or dance/movement therapist if that expertise is required.

Verbal Communication and Processing

In some instances, music therapists integrate music with verbal communication skills and verbal processing. This integration may occur to address emotional, communication, and other goals.

I noticed that your body language changed during that last song. Do you want to talk about it?

The music was really sad and made me start thinking of lonely moments in my life.

When verbal processing becomes a primary focus of the client/therapist experience, a music therapist either has received the extra formal training that allows them to work within their individual scope of practice, or consults/collaborates with a counselor or psychologist.

A crucial point here, folks! Always work within the scope of your training and abilities!

Creative Arts

Music therapists sometimes combine music with other creative arts, such as visual art or drama/theatre. For example, a music therapist might facilitate the creation of visual art (such as drawing or coloring mandalas) while listening to music, sometimes associating the two. A music therapist might also facilitate the creation of a video with music.

Depending on the selected process and outcome, as well as the music therapist's individual training and scope of practice, a music therapist may collaborate with a registered art therapist (ATR) or registered drama therapist (RDT) to strengthen the process and maintain client safety.

Let's put our expertise together to provide effective and ethical treatment!

Visuals, Manipulatives, and Props

Music therapists sometimes use books, manipulatives (such as folders that include removable visuals), and props (such as balls or stretchy bands) in their work.

These items can engage through different senses, help reinforce and structure a client's experience, and cater to people's strengths and preferences.

Summary

So, we can see how music and musicking have a lot going on!

We can also see how they connect to other arts, movement, and communication, and can be used with books, parachutes, and other props and manipulatives!

With all of this information, we are ready to talk about the general process of therapy.

You may be wondering how

The Treatment Process

is structured. Let's find out!

The Therapy (Treatment) Process

Like many healthcare professions, music therapy uses a larger treatment process to help best serve clients. The treatment process will look different in different settings, but it often includes the components shown below.

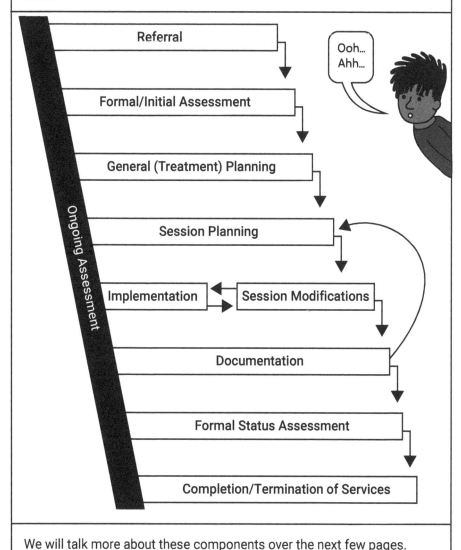

We will talk more about these components over the next few pages.

Referral

A referral is the first point of contact and the initiation that may lead to services if music therapy is a good fit.

In the case of music therapy, referrals are most likely initiated through a healthcare or educational professional, another music therapist, a caretaker, or the client themselves.

Assessment

Assessment is the process of retrieving information to better understand who a person is and where they currently are.

An assessment may include observing, interviewing (client, caretakers, healthcare professionals, others), gathering documentation, and engaging in some music therapy processes to see how a client responds to them.

When we assess, we try to understand:

• a person's strengths and needs in a range of relevant health domains
• their cultural background
• their musical background
• what resources they have or do not have available to them
• their interests and what they would like to work on.

Assessment

There are two kinds of assessment: ongoing and formal.

Ongoing assessment begins as soon as a referral happens and continues throughout the treatment process. It's probably most prominent during sessions.

During this session, I've learned about his frustration tolerance and ability to cope with challenges.

A formal assessment helps determine if music therapy is an appropriate avenue for treatment and how it can be individualized to cater to that person. If a formal assessment is required, it usually happens very early on; there can also be formal "status" assessments, which may happen every year or every few years, depending on the setting.

Assessment Types

Music therapy assessments are criterion based, meaning that they focus on the people being assessed through a set of contextual criteria, rather than how they perform based on a generalized group of peers (called norm-based or standardized assessment, such as an IQ test or standardized school assessment).

Music processes are complex and so criterion-based assessments work best.

Music therapists sometimes build assessments based on their setting, and sometimes use assessments that have already been created.

We will discuss those assessment types later in the book, in the resources section!

General (Treatment) Planning

Once we have a better understanding of who the client is and where they currently are through the assessment, we then have a better idea of what direction(s) it may be best to head in and what changes would be of benefit to their lives.

There are many paths to choose from. Based on what I've learned about you, I found a good trail for us to start on.

To begin moving in this direction, treatment planning often includes the creation of general goals and more specific objectives. Goals and objectives are often related to the health domains we discussed in our definition of music therapy (such as physiological change or changes in communication), but they can also be related to helping develop resources or changing the client's environment in some way.

Session Planning

Session planning is the process of framing and preparing what will be done in a particular session to help support a client's larger treatment plan.

We envision and create particular music processes—as based on research, our clinical expertise, and the client's experiences—in ways that can facilitate movement toward the client's goals and objectives.

One of my clients is working to reduce their anxiety. For our next session, I'll introduce them to some breathing techniques combined with calming music.

Inhale through your nose... now, hold the breath...and exhale through your mouth.

We may plan for what the specifics of the music therapy methods will look like, what the characteristics of the music may be, and what engagement, relational, and communication processes we will employ. These plans are not set in stone, but give us a starting point to work from.

Session Implementation/Modification

Honestly, no matter how much thinking and session planning we do beforehand, the session does not ever precisely happen the way we planned. As individual human beings, we are each complex, dynamic, and unique!

So, as therapists, we have to be flexible and ready to modify our music processes in the moment to match the immediate needs of the client; this is where ongoing assessment in real time becomes very important.

Documentation

Documentation can be an important part of our work, especially in particular settings. We can document during and after a session.

We can document in many ways, including, but not limited to, measuring behaviors by frequency or duration, narrating processes, and documenting client experiences as they describe them.

I write down a few notes while I'm meeting with the client. That way, I remember details about them to include in my formal documentation after the session.

I like to review my notes about my clients before I see them again. Then, I can plan my sessions more effectively.

Good documentation gives us an understanding of what worked, what did not, and what we might change in a future session.

Completion/Termination of Services

Like all other healthcare services, music therapy services at some point are completed, and our time with our client finishes.

There are many reasons to complete and terminate services, including, but not limited to, the client's needs being met, the client moving somewhere else, and the therapist not being the best fit for a particular client.

Thanks for all your help!

Because there is a transition, the therapist needs to give care and consideration to this, think ethically, and provide space for the change that will happen in the therapist-client relationship!

Music and Harm: Contraindications

Discussion on music therapy is often focused on the positive outcomes music therapy can facilitate. As with any other health profession, there is also potential for harm within a music therapy setting.

Recognizing ways in which music or the therapeutic relationship can harm is important in informing treatment decisions.

In some instances where the potential for harm is too great, music therapy may be contraindicated, meaning that music therapy or a particular therapeutic music experience may not be the best treatment for an individual.[1]

The Music Therapy and Harm Model

The Music Therapy and Harm Model (MTHM) identifies six sources of potential harm within music therapy.[2]

Music Stimulus

Music Therapist

Application of Music Interventions

Therapeutic Relationship

Client Associations with Music

Ecological Factors

Examples of Contraindications in Music Therapy[3]

A neurodivergent individual with sensory sensitivity being unable to tolerate certain frequencies or timbres.

A music therapist lacking adequate training in an area of work, or working outside their scope of practice.

Playing certain sounds or songs associated with negative experiences that happened in a client's life.

Let's discover some

Therapeutic Music Experiences

that music therapists may implement in their practice.

Re-creation

The first method we will discuss is re-creation.[1] Re-creation involves the client learning or performing an existing piece of music, either in part or in full. Music re-creation can occur using vocalizations, instruments, or a combination of both, and can occur with or without an audience. Re-creation may look like a patient singing along to a song with a music therapist, a group playing a familiar song together on various instruments, or a client learning to play a new instrument.

Composition

The second method we will discuss is composition.[2] Music composition is a form of creating a new piece of music through writing lyrics, creating instrumental parts, creating a musical product like a recording or video, or a combination of these.

Songwriting is a common form of composition in music therapy, and can be approached in many different ways. Let's take a look at some different songwriting approaches.

Piggyback Songwriting

Piggyback songwriting is a technique where new lyrics are written to an existing melody. This style is approachable for those new to songwriting, and can create songs that are easy to remember and align with client-preferred musical genres.[3]

Fill-in-the-Blank Songwriting

Fill-in-the-blank songwriting uses the structure of a selected song, where blanks are inserted and the client creates their own responses to create the song. This provides a structure for those who may be new to songwriting while still creating the opportunity for choice and self-expression.[4]

Example (to "Flowers" by Miley Cyrus):

I can _snuggle with my dog_

Write _about how I feel_

Talk to _my best friend on the phone_

Say _affirmations to myself_

I can _practice deep breathing_

And I can _walk by the dam_

Yeah, I can love me better than others can.

Spot Songwriting

Spot songwriting, also called extemporaneous songwriting and free songwriting, is a form of songwriting where both the melody and lyrics of a song are original. Stylistic elements and chord progressions may be similar to other songs, but no pre-set structure is used. This type of songwriting may be completed in a single session or treated as a long-term project.

Spot songwriting allows for the most flexibility and personalization, but also provides less structure than other forms.[5] The process for spot songwriting may vary, but often involves identifying elements or phrases to include and piecing them together with a desired beat or chord progression.

Blues Songwriting

Twelve-bar blues is a great form for composing lyrics, because the lyrical form can be made simple while also creative and powerful. If you listen to blues songs like "Kansas City" by Leiber and Stoller, or "Crossroads" by Robert Johnson, or "Give Me One Reason to Stay Here" by Tracy Chapman, or "Jump, Jive, an' Wail" by Louis Prima, you can hear this lyrical form in action!

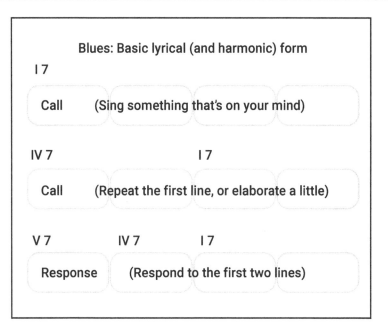

Blues: Basic lyrical (and harmonic) form

I 7

Call   (Sing something that's on your mind)

IV 7   I 7

Call   (Repeat the first line, or elaborate a little)

V 7   IV 7   I 7

Response   (Respond to the first two lines)

Through this link, you can view a music therapy session where the blues form is being used for improvising.

www.youtube.com/watch?v=NLuvEwu_dew

Instrumental Composition

Music therapists may also facilitate clients composing music with instruments. Any instrument, including electronic and computer-based instruments, can be used. The composing process can be made as accessible as needed to promote success.

Improvisational Methods

Improvisation, as a music therapy method, often promotes creativity and personal expression in the moment. However, music therapists often use and sometimes even plan supportive frames and forms, such as chord progressions and rhythmic support. That way, clients feel comfortable trying things musically. There are also many techniques in clinical improvisation that music therapists use to support, validate, guide, and interact with clients.

Improvisational Methods

www.youtube.com/watch?v=UOrDoXPaNpw

www.youtube.com/watch?v=DSbp0Ffqvm8

Here are some video examples of music therapy improvisation!

www.youtube.com/watch?v=esAYtvA7EuI

www.youtube.com/watch?v=ow_nGPi3d9k

Receptive Methods

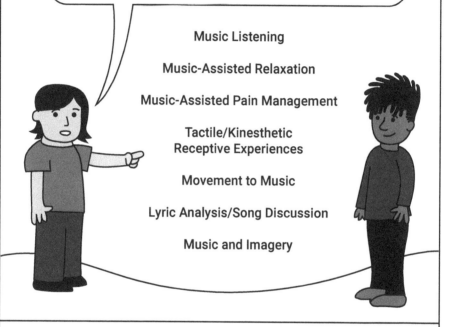

As we've talked about before, receiving music is commonly thought of as engaging through listening, but can also include other types of sensory input. These are some therapeutic music experiences related to receptive methods.

Music Listening

Music-Assisted Relaxation

Music-Assisted Pain Management

Tactile/Kinesthetic Receptive Experiences

Movement to Music

Lyric Analysis/Song Discussion

Music and Imagery

Let's discuss each of these a little bit more!

Music Listening

Music listening is an umbrella process that may be used for many reasons and to address different goals. Sometimes music listening may be used for calming or meditative purposes, while other times it may be used for stimulation, movement, orientation, and many other purposes. Music listening can incorporate prompts for action like a movement or verbal response, as in the example below.[6]

Music-Assisted Relaxation

Music-assisted relaxation processes focus on the receiving of music (usually listening) with the intention of promoting relaxation, reducing stress, and/or reducing anxiety. In many cases, these types of therapeutic processes incorporate music listening with a verbal script.

The music provides a background and reinforces the verbally guided process. The script may include, but not be limited to, a focus on breathing, progressive muscle relaxation (the tensing and releasing of muscle groups across the body), or mindfulness of the body. The music tends to be relatively predictable while maintaining interest. The therapist takes into account the characteristics of music, and, if playing music live, may change them in the moment in response to the client.

Music-Assisted Pain Management

In some cases, music therapists use music in a way that is related to relaxation but more specific. During or after some medical procedures, we can experience pain.

A music therapist may work with a client during or after a medical procedure, using music listening or music making as a way to distract from the perception of pain: for example, when people are getting an intravenous device placed, or when having dressings changed for a burn.

Tactile/Kinesthetic Receptive Experiences

We can feel vibrations when we stand next to a large speaker or play a large drum. We can also feel the physical feedback of many instruments as we play them. There are even chairs and mattresses that can vibrate with the frequencies of music as it plays.

Instruments like the singing bowl, steel tongue drum, paddle drums, and kalimba offer receptive sensory experiences when played, and can help with a client's sensory grounding in order to regulate their body, or provide sensory stimulation for someone who needs more sensory input. Music therapists strategically use tactile and kinesthetic feedback to music to address clients' varying sensory needs and interests.

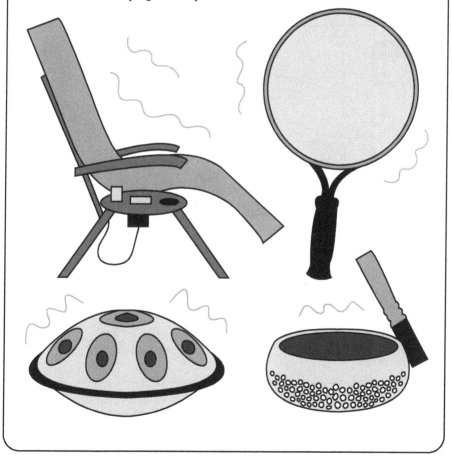

Movement to Music

When we listen to music, we sometimes move to it in our own unique way. It's more physically engaging than just "receiving" the music, making it an active response to the receptive experience. Movement and dance are uniquely expressive, and are inseparable from much music around the world. In a music therapy session, the music therapist may facilitate movement experiences with the body, sometimes including props like scarves or parachutes.

The music is carefully chosen or created to reflect the desired movements and motions. Movement can be reflected through the various characteristics of the music, including the lyrics.

Lyric Analysis/Song Discussion

We often listen to songs because they communicate meaning to us through the lyrics and other characteristics. Themes about relationships, struggles, empowerment, grieving, and many other topics can be found in songs. Songs can be analyzed and discussed to further probe into how their meanings relate to us. Music therapists work to contain analysis and discussion to promote growth while maintaining a feeling of safety.[7]

Music and Imagery

Many people, to varying degrees, receive music in ways that can result in "visual" images in their minds. Music and imagery is a psychodynamic receptive music experience that facilitates clients in further engaging with their imagery, and potentially other sensory responses.

Music therapists, at their level of advanced training, may facilitate imagery for supportive and re-educative processes. They carefully select music and consider the best way to promote, structure, and guide the imagery process, such as through drawing, verbal communication, and verbal interpretation. Facilitation focuses on the client's autonomy and safety.

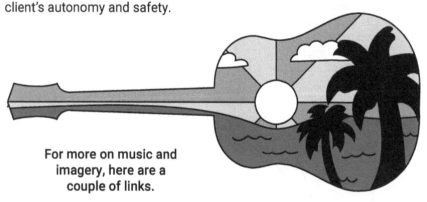

For more on music and imagery, here are a couple of links.

https://ami-bonnymethod.org

Association for
Music & Imagery

https://vimeo.com/3130402

A music therapist sharing
their own experience of a
guided imagery process

Introducing Theories and Approaches to Practice

Because music therapy is so diverse, there are many ways it can be practiced. Some approaches originated in other fields like psychology and music education, while others are indigenous to the field of music therapy.

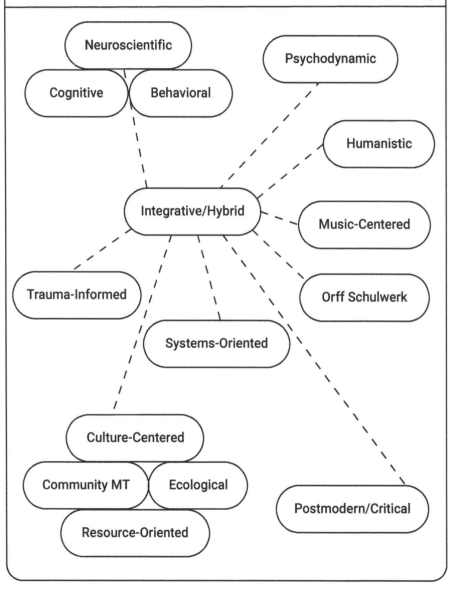

Neuroscientifically Informed Approaches

Like many other healthcare fields, music therapy has increasingly looked at how the brain works: in our case, how music and the brain interact with each other.

Similarly, practitioners in the field of neuroscience have also increased their curiosity about music. Studies have shown how music can be uniquely situated to create new neural pathways that can facilitate movement, emotional regulation, and communication, among other areas.

Some great examples can be seen in the following videos and study abstract:

www.youtube.com/watch?v=TQi7btgt_fw

Communication

www.youtube.com/watch?v=cq8fv3Hpoao

Movement

https://pubmed.ncbi.nlm.nih.gov/24568004

Emotional Regulation

Behavioral Approaches

Behavioral approaches focus primarily on how music experiences may help people modify behaviors. These approaches take into account what influences the behavior shortly beforehand, during, and shortly afterwards. From the behavioral perspective, music can motivate, structure, and reinforce processes.

Clinicians, for example, may work on promoting particular cognitive behaviors (such as attending to a task), particular social behaviors (such as sharing and greeting), or particular daily living tasks (such as tying a shoe lace, brushing teeth, or using money).

Work on behaviors can be seen as an opportunity to help people navigate the world, but should also be ethically considered and appropriately individualized for each client.[1]

Cognitive-Behavioral Approaches

Cognitive-behavioral approaches focus on helping people identify and alter disturbing thought patterns that negatively influence behaviors. The focus for the clinician and client is on treatment of current thoughts, behaviors, and physical responses, and not what has happened in the past; instead they explore how these recent or present thoughts, feelings, and actions are all interrelated and can impact one another.[2]

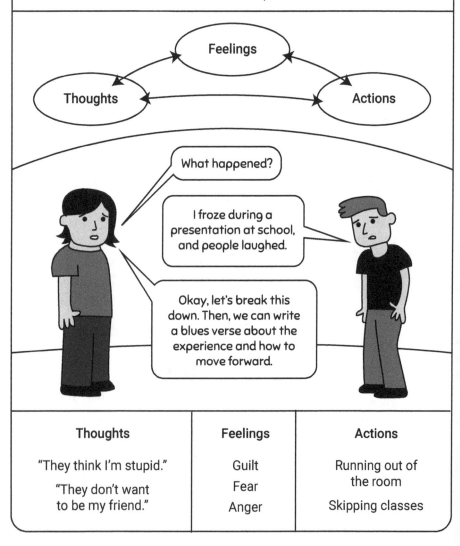

Thoughts	Feelings	Actions
"They think I'm stupid."	Guilt	Running out of the room
"They don't want to be my friend."	Fear	Skipping classes
	Anger	

Developmental Approaches

During our lifespan we all develop in many areas. Healthcare professionals in a range of fields have put together theories of development for sensory, cognitive, emotional, social, and other domains. These theories continue to evolve over time as we learn more. Each of us develops differently and on different timelines, but there can be similarities in that development as well. Developmental music therapy approaches take one or more of these theories and trajectories into account, often asking how music can facilitate growth in a particular developmental area.[3]

For example, a person develops their fine motor (grasping) skills by first learning how to hold a ball or large shaker (spherical grasp) and then how to use more closed grasps with smaller items (like an egg shaker), and then more detailed grasps with individual fingers (such as a three jaw chuck hold on a triangle striker). These skills build (or in some cases re-build) someone's ability to grasp objects, to write with a pencil, and so on.

Make the bunny ears... then cross the middle... then what?

Another example we can use is psychologist Jean Piaget's developmental process of learning a task, and how it relates to independent competence, confidence, and creativity. We often begin learning a task (such as tying a shoelace or playing an instrument) by breaking it down into smaller tasks and imitating particular actions that we see or read. As we get more comfortable, we put the entire task together in relation to our own way of doing things, even adding our own style to it.

These are just two of many examples of development!

Psychodynamic

Psychodynamic approaches grew out of psychoanalysis, but evolved to focus more on empathy and client interaction. Psychodynamic approaches in music therapy try to better understand and address the "hows" and "whys" of a particular need, challenge, thought process, or behavior, often through exploring both conscious and unconscious processes that happen within music engagement.

As basic examples: music therapists may facilitate a referential improvisation (where people express an idea like the weather or a feeling) with clients, or they may facilitate the analysis of lyrics to a song to understand personal meanings, or they may safely explore how music can promote imagery for clients.[4] Music therapists may also collaborate with counselors and psychologists in this regard.

We can use these drums to express emotions. Do you have an emotion in mind that we can represent by using rhythm, tempo, and volume?

Yeah! I already have an idea for anger. I think it needs to have an erratic rhythm with a fast tempo, and of course...super loud!

Humanistic

Humanistic approaches in psychology, and healthcare in general, arose to address needs that behavioral approaches, the medical model, and psychoanalysis did not focus on. Humanism rejected what it saw as the deterministic approaches of the past, instead focusing on the capacity of the human being.

Characteristics of humanistic approaches include unconditional positive regard, empathy, an emphasis on a person's strengths, self-actualization, and creativity. Music, as a primarily human endeavor that fosters creativity, can be affirming, empowering, and self-actualizing. A humanistic approach capitalizes on these endeavors.

Orff Schulwerk

Orff Schulwerk is a children's music education approach developed by Carl Orff and Gunild Keetman. The approach uses chanting, music, movement, and storytelling in developmentally accessible ways to help children joyfully engage in and learn about music.

The accessibility of Orff Schulwerk ideas and instrumentation can align well with music therapy processes. Gertrud Orff helped to develop the crossover from education to health.[5]

Music-Centered Approaches

Music-centered approaches to music therapy focus primarily on the shared music experiences between therapist and client(s)/participants, the power of musical creativity, the uniqueness of musical processes, and the musical outcomes that result. Underlying this focus is the idea that the value and power of music always belongs to the music making itself (and the people making it), including when considered for the purposes of promoting health.

Systems-Oriented Approaches

In general, systems theories emphasize that change often occurs through the interdependence between different components, whether they be human, human made, or of the natural world. Systems can be related to physics, physiology (such as the nervous system), and social structures/institutions.

Music can be seen as a way, or even as a unique creative technology, to promote interaction between people and the systems around them. Some resources for understanding a few approaches to systems theory include Crowe[6] and Schneck and Berger,[7] as well as the ways that music therapists have incorporated the developmental systems work of Bronfenbrenner.[8]

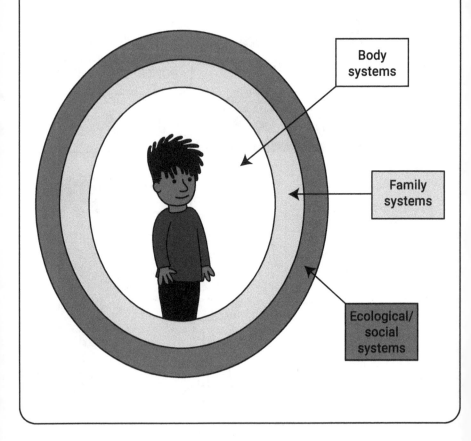

Body systems

Family systems

Ecological/ social systems

Culturally and Ecologically Informed Approaches[9]

Like any of the arts (e.g. visual, dance, culinary), music can be understood as a set of diverse culturally and ecologically situated practices. The instruments and sounds created in music originate from people, their practices, and their environmental surroundings. Some approaches in music therapy place primary focus on the way the client, the therapist, and the music are culturally and ecologically situated.

Culture in this sense is not just ethnic or racial, but related to all aspects of each individual: what makes them unique and what allows them to connect to others on a daily basis. To some degree, these approaches can be seen intersecting with systems-oriented approaches, but may also be more focused on social, cultural, and political systems.

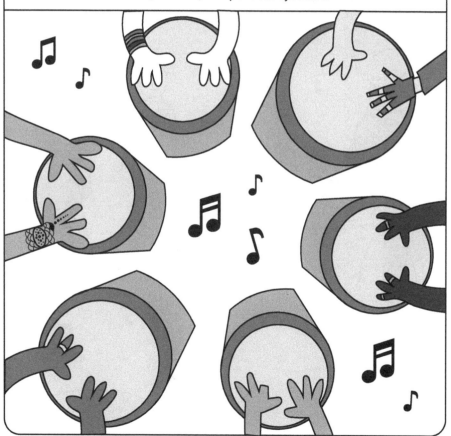

Community Music Therapy Approaches

Music, or perhaps better stated, musicking (the act of making music), can allow you to share with others your value, uniqueness, and potential, either individually or in a group (or both!). Music has a long history of promoting cultural values and changing social structures. Community music therapy can be understood as a culturally informed approach to music therapy. However, it is prevalent enough that it deserves its own description.

Community Music Therapy Approaches

Community music therapy approaches seek to use music in situated ways to promote social change, empowering individuals and groups through music making, challenging perceptions about abilities, and changing community and institutional structures. Examples of community music therapy include, but are not limited to, community drumming and/or singing events, as well as inclusive performing ensembles.

Resource-Oriented Approaches

Resource-oriented music therapy is an approach that focuses on promoting positive experiences, strengths, current resources, and access to new resources in order to empower people.[10] Therapists using this approach are highly collaborative in their relationship with clients. This approach can readily connect with culture-centered, community-oriented, and humanistic approaches, as well as with self-determination theory. This approach has existed in some form since the beginning of the profession, but is now more developed and specific, particularly in mental health care.

A simple example, although one that can become very complex and layered, is learning to play an instrument. The approach that the therapist and client take together is much more collaborative than a traditional piano lesson. If interest is initiated by a client to learn/play, the piano and music give space and access to the collaboration, through which engagement and growth can occur.

Postmodern/Poststructural/Critical Approaches

The terms "postmodern" and "poststructural" are philosophical umbrellas that cover many different ways of looking at ourselves in the world—each of these ways challenging or seeing alternatives to commonly established ways of thinking and doing, whether they manifest in traditions, language, institutions, or actions.

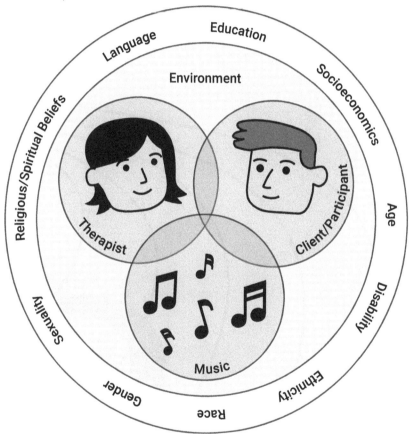

These approaches sometimes see health problems as problems of access and power, and seek to empower people and change social structures/systems. There can be connection to cultural, community-oriented, and resource-oriented approaches, but this approach may center more directly on privilege, disadvantage, and social change.

Trauma-Informed Music Therapy

Trauma-informed music therapy is a more recent approach that grew out of other general trauma-informed healthcare practices. This approach is commonly used in mental health settings where people have experienced acute or long-term traumatic events, but the approach crosses over to all populations and settings.

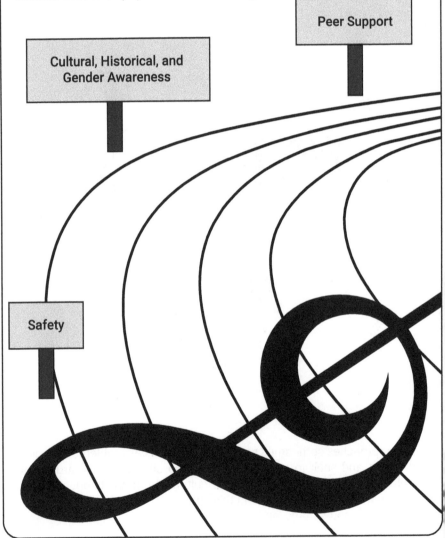

Peer Support

Cultural, Historical, and Gender Awareness

Safety

Hybrid, Contextually Informed, and Integrative Approaches

As in many fields, music therapy practitioners do not rely on only one theory or approach to inform their work. There are many rationales for combining ideas from different approaches. First, some approaches are already connected. Second, different contexts or settings may expose limitations to a single approach; in those instances, moving to another approach or using ideas from another approach can address those limitations.

Often, clinicians who have practiced for years feel comfortable enough in their own depth with one approach that they add to their own personal style by being informed by multiple approaches.[11]

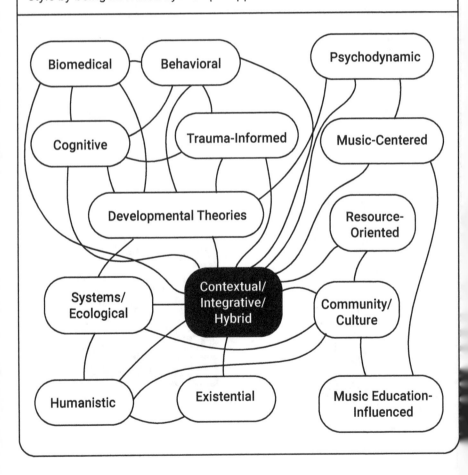

Music Therapy, Populations, and Settings

Music therapists work with many different people in many different settings. Sometimes, music therapists work with clients individually, and at other times in groups. There are a number of different settings where music therapists work too. Let's explore some of these settings and populations to learn more about what music therapy can look like.

Don't forget that just about anyone can participate in music therapy. Music therapists work with people from birth through to the end of life, and musical experience or ability is not required to participate. All genres of music can be used in music therapy, and the music therapist uses the client's preferred music to inform their sessions. These examples are just the beginning of what music therapy sessions look like!

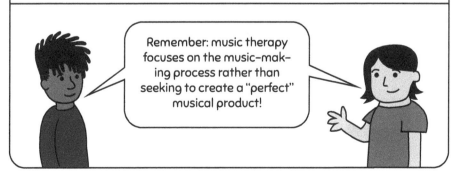

Music Therapy in Mental Health

Mental health refers to emotional and psychological well-being, affecting behaviors, feelings, and thoughts.

It can be helpful to think of mental health as a spectrum and that everyone falls somewhere on it.

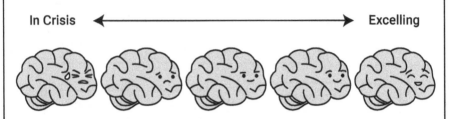

When there are clinically significant changes in behaviors, feelings, or thoughts, this can signal that a mental health condition is present.

Mental health conditions are often diagnosed by a licensed psychologist or psychiatrist, who are specially trained to identify nuances of symptoms and diagnoses of mental illness. Most music therapists treat clients with mental health conditions after they have been diagnosed by a licensed healthcare provider.

Music Therapy in Mental Health

It is important for music therapists to recognize diagnosed mental health conditions as clinical definitions of what a client may be experiencing and not as a definition of the client.

Music Therapy in Mental Health

Music therapists serve clients of all ages with mental health needs in a variety of settings, including inpatient psychiatric settings, correctional settings, community settings, rehabilitation settings, residential settings, and private practice.[2]

In 2018, approximately 19% of music therapists in the U.S. reported that they worked with people with mental health and substance use conditions.[1]

Music Therapy in Mental Health [3] [4] [5] [6]

Music therapists work with individuals on mental health goals in many settings. In a group setting, one common goal area is increasing social skills and building empathy, which may be addressed through an intervention like clinical improvisation. Individuals can also develop creative coping skills, such as learning to play an instrument to build distress tolerance, mastery, and self-esteem.

Common goal areas:

· Increase sense of self-esteem
· Decrease stress
· Implement healthy coping strategies in daily life
· Increase effective communication and social engagement
· Increase motivation

Developmental Disabilities

Developmental disabilities is an umbrella term that refers to both intellectual and physical disabilities that may compromise someone's developmental trajectory in various domains (e.g. physical, cognitive, communication, emotional, social). Music therapists may work with people to help with these areas of development, while also creating environments that are accessible and provide people with space to be themselves in music.

For example, regarding physical development, music and musical instruments can be used to help practice visual tracking and auditory tracking, as well as articulation of speech sounds.

With intellectual development, music therapists can facilitate music experiences that promote attending for longer periods of time, recognizing colors, letters, and words, and practicing the use of money or other activities of daily living.

Neurodivergence

Neurodivergence refers to people whose brains develop or work differently from what is considered "typical," resulting in different ways of processing sensory input and information. Neurodivergence can therefore also be seen as a spectrum of unique strengths and challenges that a person may have within the environments they navigate on a daily basis.

Some diagnoses that may be considered under the umbrella of neurodivergence include, but are not limited to, autism, attention deficit hyperactivity disorder, dyslexia, and synesthesia.

Music is a unique mode of sensory input, processing, communication, and social interaction. This uniqueness can make music therapy a powerful fit with some neurodivergent people.

Special Education

Some music therapists work in schools, under the umbrella of special education, with other healthcare professionals (such as speech language pathologists, physical therapists, and occupational therapists) as well as with teachers.

> The purpose of healthcare professionals in education is to help students reach their educational goals.

Music therapists may work under an Individualized Education Plan for students, or may consult with teachers and other professionals to provide music strategies that can help with areas including, but not limited to: learning academic fundamentals (e.g. color and letter recognition), cognitive development (e.g. attention, sequencing), sensory awareness, motor skills (e.g. those that will help someone to write with pencils or use technology, but will also promote physical health), emotional awareness and regulation, social development, and individual and group problem solving.

Medical

Some music therapists work in hospitals. They use music to support patients and their families during a hospital stay. Music therapists can work with patients all over the hospital, but we will look at a few specific examples of music therapy in a hospital setting.

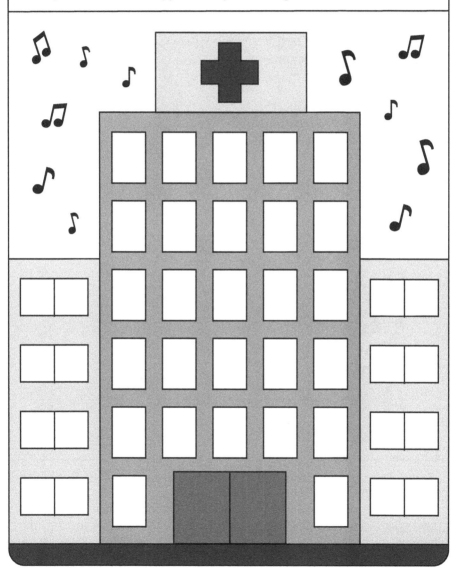

Obstetrics

Music therapy assisted childbirth (MTACB)

Common goal areas:[7]

· Reduce pain and tension
· Assist movement
· Improve physical comfort
· Provide a sense of security
· Reduce anxiety and fear
· Improve mental focus
· Provide emotional comfort
· Increase feelings of control
· Facilitate bonding for all involved
  in the birthing process

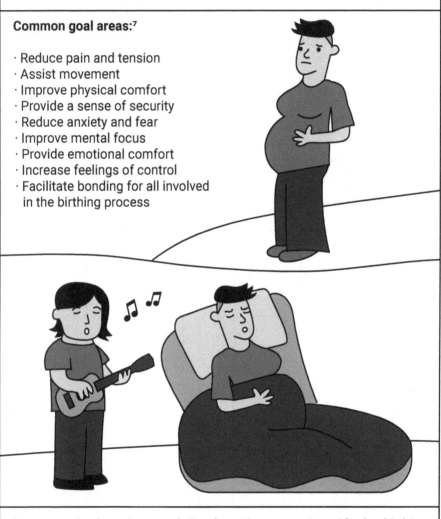

Some music therapists work in obstetrics to assist with the birthing process. They may use familiar music to create a comfortable environment and provide a stimulus to distract the person in labor. Music therapists may also pair music with relaxation techniques to calm the person in labor.

Procedural Support

Sometimes, a music therapist may be present to help a patient cope with a medical procedure like an IV placement or a wound dressing change. This may include providing an interactive musical experience to redirect attention or a receptive musical experience to promote calming. This is called procedural support, and is used to reduce distress caused by the procedure.[8]

Intensive Care Units (ICUs)

Common goal areas:

· Reduce perception of pain
· Reduce anxiety and stress[9]
· Provide psychosocial support to the patient and family
· Provide sensory stimulation
· Process emotions surrounding illness/injury[10]

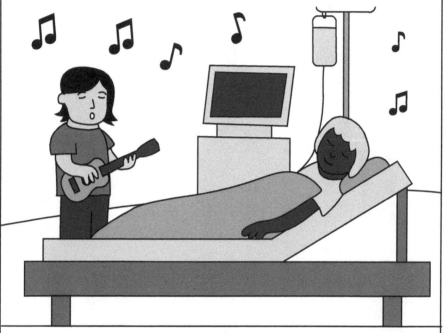

Some music therapists work in hospital intensive care units (ICUs). ICUs treat critically ill patients and are often stressful environments for patients and families.

In an ICU setting, music therapists may work with patients recovering from major surgery, receiving care for burns, or patients who are mechanically ventilated. These patients may have altered states of consciousness and high levels of pain, so music therapists may use music-assisted relaxation techniques to calm patients, or songwriting techniques to help the patient and family process their emotions.[11]

Cancer Care/Oncology

Common goal areas:

· Improve coping with diagnosis and treatment
· Help patients adapt to the treatment environment[12]
· Provide opportunity for emotional expression through music
· Reduce pain
· Improve functional skills
· Provide grief support for patients and families[13]

Music therapists also work with people receiving cancer treatments. Because cancer treatments are often long term, a music therapist may work with the same patients multiple times throughout the course of their treatment. The music therapist will plan their sessions to fit the patient's individual situation, especially based on whether the treatment is curative, chronic, or palliative in nature.[13]

For patients with curative treatments, music therapists may focus more on improving skills that may have been affected by cancer progression and medical treatments. Patients receiving treatment for chronic illness may need more assistance for adapting to the treatment environment and expressing emotions related to chronic illness. For patients receiving palliative treatments, the sessions may focus more on pain management and coping with their prognosis.

Neonatal Intensive Care Unit (NICU)

Common goal areas:[14]

· Increase non-nutritive sucking
· Increase tolerance to
  multimodal stimulation
· Regulate behavior state
· Regulate respiration rate
  and oxygen saturation

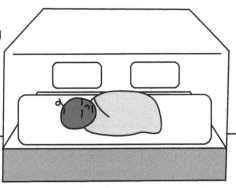

Music therapists also work with premature infants in the neonatal intensive care unit, known as the NICU. Premature infants require additional time and assistance to grow and develop. Music therapists use techniques like multimodal stimulation to increase an infant's tolerance to environmental stimuli and improve self-regulation skills.

Additionally, music therapists may use tools like a pacifier-activated lullaby to encourage non-nutritive sucking behaviors and regulate an infant's emotional state following painful medical procedures.

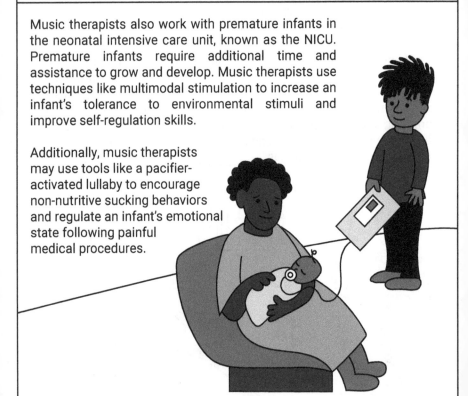

Neonatal Intensive Care Unit (NICU)

Some approaches in the NICU also focus on addressing the inter-related needs of the parents/caretakers and the child. A music therapist may play a role in helping parents learn, gain resources, and, most importantly, form a healthy bond with the child that will influence future development. This family-centered care can reduce the negative effects of prolonged hospitalization on the parent-infant relationship.[15]

The music therapist may support parents in singing lullabies and songs of kin to soothe and bond with their child.[16]

Correctional Settings

Music therapists often work in different types of correctional settings. Music therapists' roles in each setting are similar (often with a focus on rehabilitative mental health), but also slightly different (amount of time to work with people, ages/development, types of rehabilitation/educational focus).

Jails:
People awaiting trial or generally shorter-term stay for adults

Prisons:
Longer-term setting

Juvenile detention centers:
Generally shorter-term for children and adolescents

Juvenile correctional facilities:
Generally longer-term for children and adolescents

Forensic hospitals:
Psychiatric facilities where individuals may go for mental health treatment during their sentencing process.

Older Adults

Music therapists work with older adults in a variety of settings and with varying goals, including the following:[17]

> Health and Well-Being Settings

> Intergenerational Programming

> Alzheimer's Disease and Memory Care

> Hospice and Palliative Care

Health and Well-Being

Common goal areas:

· Maintain physical fitness through coordination, balance, flexibility, and range of motion
· Maintain cognitive acuity
· Promote self-worth
· Develop techniques for emotional expression
· Build social support networks

Health and Well-Being Playlist

▶

▶ Physical Fitness ⋯
▶ Cognition ⋯
▶ Self-Worth ⋯
▶ Social Health ⋯
▶ Emotional Expression ⋯
▶ Stress Management ⋯

Music therapy is sometimes used in programs to promote overall wellness rather than addressing a specific area of need. These programs take a preventative approach toward maintaining health through physical fitness, cognitive health, emotional and social support, and stress management by reinforcing behaviors that promote health and well-being. Music therapy for wellness often occurs in group settings over extended periods of time, where participants develop socially supportive relationships.[18]

Health and Well-Being

In practice, this may look like a music therapist leading a movement-based program set to musical cues to promote physical fitness goals like maintaining balance and range of motion.

To promote cognitive skills and coordination, a music therapist may facilitate group musical experiences that involve rhythmic or melodic patterns that increase in complexity and incorporate use of short-term memory.

To promote self-worth and self-expression, music therapists may facilitate songwriting or performance experiences to provide opportunities for creative self-expression.[19]

Intergenerational Programming

Intergenerational programming seeks to reduce age segregation, which is prevalent in modern Western society. Many families are generationally separated, which limits opportunities for intergenerational interaction. Intergenerational music therapy settings can include older participants serving younger participants by singing songs with educational content to assist in their learning.

Younger participants can also serve older participants through use of music technology and education of newer musical trends. Both younger and older participants can teach the group about songs from their generations. Most importantly, intergenerational music therapy programming involves shared musical engagement through instrument play, singing, or both.[20]

Common goal areas:

· Provide opportunities for social interaction
· Decrease isolation
· Improve attitude toward aging
· Improve life satisfaction

Dementia and Memory Care

Music therapists often work with people with Alzheimer's disease and other types of dementia. This type of care often occurs in memory care facilities and skilled nursing facilities, although it can also be offered in client homes if they receive in-home care. Clients with dementia face cognitive decline, confusion, and communication difficulties, which can lead to disruptive behaviors like wandering, verbal aggression, and physical aggression. Additionally, their caregivers may experience psychological stress, financial stress, fatigue, and social isolation.

As we have seen in other types of music therapy work, music therapists working in memory care may address both client and caregiver needs. This may look like a music therapist performing meaningful live music to inspire life reflection, incorporating familiar and preferred music into routines to reduce agitation, and utilizing instrument play to preserve flexibility and strength.

Common goal areas:[21]

· Encourage reminiscence
· Provide opportunity for meaningful patient and caregiver interaction
· Provide familiar and comforting stimuli for orientation
· Reduce agitation, verbal aggression, physical aggression, and wandering

Hospice and Palliative Care

Music therapists in hospice care work with patients nearing the end of their life. Hospice care is provided when a patient or their decision-maker chooses to stop pursuing treatment for a serious illness. It often involves treating the patient's symptoms without treating the root cause. In this setting, music therapists may work with patients and their families to provide psychosocial support and preserve quality of life. Hospice care is often provided in private homes and long-term care facilities, but is also offered in hospitals and hospices.

Similarly, palliative care is an approach to treat symptoms of illness or side effects of treatment while patients are often still undergoing treatment for serious illness. The music therapy goals in palliative care may be similar, although the patient may not necessarily have a terminal illness or be approaching the end of their life.[22]

Common goal areas:

· Cope with serious illness
· Express thoughts and feelings
· Facilitate interactions between patient and family[23]
· Reduce perception of pain
· Promote relaxation
· Reduce anxiety[24]

Community-Based Work

Earlier, we talked about community music therapy as a theoretical orientation. Some music therapists do community-based work, sometimes because the setting itself is community-based. This type of music therapy focuses on collaborative music making within a given community rather than focusing on a specific population or need.[25]

There are a lot of ways community work might look, but some examples include facilitating community drumming, creating bands with a Boys and Girls Club, or offering group piano lessons to older adults.

Refugees

Refugees are people who have been forced to leave their country for various reasons, including natural disasters, persecution, and war. These experiences are often traumatic and can leave refugees more vulnerable to experiencing mental health conditions.

While these traumatic events can affect all people, children and adolescents in particular are at higher risk for reduced psychosocial support. Music therapy can provide both behavioral and psychological benefits for refugees in individual and group work.

One common goal area for music therapy with refugees is connection to culture. We might also focus on improving emotional regulation and emotional expression.

Some other common goal areas are decreasing behavioral difficulties, improving self-expression, and enhancing interactions with others.[26]

Military Service Members and Veterans

Some music therapists work with military members and veterans in settings like Veterans Affairs Centers or local community health clinics. Services may be provided to individuals in all military service branches and may extend to service members' families and children.[27]

Music therapy goals range widely from focusing on physical or neurological goals related to injuries in combat to mental health goals related to psychological trauma sustained while on duty.

To hear more about music therapy with this population, watch this video!

www.youtube.com/watch?v=MRsDed44dEM

Summary

We've covered quite a few different populations and settings in which music therapists work, but there are more populations and settings out there that music therapists currently serve and that we will serve in the future.

Music therapists are also changing the ways they connect with clients, including the use of telehealth services.

How to Find a Music Therapist (US and International)

To find a music therapist in the United States, you can go to this webpage.

www.musictherapy.org/about/find

In the United States and internationally, one way you can find music therapists is through a webpage at the Certification Board for Music Therapists.

https://my.cbmt.org/cbmtssa/f?p=CRTSSA:17800:7860262722622:::17800::

In the UK, you can use the following webpage at the British Association for Music Therapy.

www.bamt.org/resources/find-a-therapist

You can also look at websites of associations in other countries to contact them for information.

Music Therapy Training

You can find a list of places to study music therapy in the United States here…

https://netforum.avectra.com/eweb/DynamicPage.aspx?Site=AMTA2&WebCode=OrgResult&FromSearchControl=Yes

…and you can find a list of places to study music therapy in Europe here!

https://emtc-eu.com/training/training-programs

Music Therapy Journals

Journal of Music Therapy

https://academic.oup.com/jmt

Music Therapy Perspectives

https://academic.oup.com/mtp

These are some music therapy journals that require a subscription.

Nordic Journal of Music Therapy

www.tandfonline.com/toc/rnjm20/current

Music Therapy Journals

British Journal of Music Therapy

https://journals.sagepub.com/home/bjm

The Arts in Psychotherapy

www.sciencedirect.com/journal/
the-arts-in-psychotherapy

Go on, check out these journals. I double dog dare you!

Australian Journal of Music Therapy

www.austmta.org.au/consumers-resources/ajmt-journal

Music Therapy Journals

Voices

www.voices.no

Approaches

https://approaches.gr

And here are some open access journals! Check 'em out!

Dialogues in Music Therapy Education

https://journals.iupui.edu/index.php/dmte/about

Some Other Introductory Books in Music Therapy

There are MANY books about music therapy. We offer just a few books that give an overview of the field, as well as provide a resource to look at more specialized books below!

Defining Music Therapy
by Kenneth Bruscia

Music Therapy: An Introduction to the Profession
by Andrew Knight, Blythe Lagasse, and Alicia Clair

Music Therapy Handbook
by Barbara Wheeler

Music Heard So Deeply: A Music Therapy Memoir
by Betsey King

Music therapy books published by Jessica Kingsley Publishers can be found here!

Jessica Kingsley
Publishers

https://uk.jkp.com/collections/music-therapy-arts-therapies-pid-1007

Assessment Tools

SEMTAP   IMTAP

MATADOC

IMCAP-ND   MiDAS

There is a bit of literature on music therapy assessment,[1] including quite a few types of formal assessments that exist in music therapy.

If you are interested, let's discuss some of those assessment types here.

SEMTAP²

The Special Education Music Therapy Assessment Process, or SEMTAP, is commonly used in special education settings to see if music therapy services may be a necessary part of a student's individualized education plan. In order to qualify for music therapy services in special education, a student demonstrates significant improvement in academic objectives through music interventions, when compared with their standard educational setting.

For example, a student who may have difficulty identifying colors may be more successful using the melody of music, as employed by a music therapist through a composed song, to reinforce that identification in a way that classroom strategies have not worked.

The assessment uses formal observation in classroom settings, review of prior documentation, and music therapy intervention sessions to provide this comparison. If music appears to facilitate significant improvement through the assessment, then the music therapist can recommend services to the student's support team (parents/caregivers, other therapists, teachers, and administrators) during a formal meeting.

IMTAP[3]

The Individualized Music Therapy Assessment Profile is a global assessment originally created for use in pediatric and adolescent settings. It is useful for those working with people with a range of needs and diagnoses, and within various settings.

The IMTAP was developed by Holly Tuesday Baxter, Julie Allis Berghofer, Lesa MacEwan, Judy Nelson, Kasi Peters, and Penny Roberts. Check out the book!

IMCAP-ND[4]

The Individual Music-Centered Assessment Profile for Neurodevelopmental Disorders, or IMCAP-ND, is an assessment process that takes into account specific music demonstration, including musical attention, music perception, and musical responsiveness.

Assessment Tools: MATADOC[5]

The Music Assessment Tool for Awareness in Disorders of Consciousness focuses on assessing those who have levels of consciousness (e.g. coma, minimal consciousness), often occurring due to trauma, reduced oxygen or blood supply to the brain, or poisoning.

Even with changes in consciousness, people can process things from the environment, including sounds; they can therefore be receptive to sound and music. Assessment of that reception requires knowledge of what to observe.

MiDAS[6]

The Music in Dementia Assessment Scales tool focuses on people who have dementia. The tool uses a visual analog scale in five areas: levels of interest, response, initiation, involvement, and enjoyment. These scales can then be quantified, and combined with narrative information on interactions.

We hope you have learned something new about the field of music therapy, and how music can relate to health. The work of music therapists is continually developing to meet the needs of our changing world. The field continues to publish substantial research while also learning to do so in even more rigorous ways.

Each music therapist is unique because of our musical and personal backgrounds. We are also connected to each other through a larger intention to promote healthy ways of living and spaces/times for our own music to thrive. We all want to thank you for reading through!

Goodbye!

Endnotes by Chapter

Introduction

1. This idea of music in everyday life has been discussed by musicologist Tia DeNora, in her book by the same name: De Nora, T. (2000). *Music in Everyday Life*. Cambridge University Press.
2. Wikimedia Foundation. (2023, January 6). *Writing about music is like dancing about architecture*. Wikipedia. https://en.wikipedia.org/wiki/Writing_about_music_is_like_ dancing_about_architecture
3. This definition is largely attributed to Bruscia, in Bruscia, K. E. (2014). *Defining Music Therapy*. Barcelona. We have made minor modifications and additions.
4. Find more information about board certification here: www.cbmt.org
5. www.musictherapy.org/about/requirements
6. www.bamt.org/music-therapy/what-is-a-music-therapist
7. www.austmta.org.au/about-us/how-to-become-an-rmt
8. Matney, B. (2007). *Tataku: The Use of Percussion in Music Therapy*. Sarsen Publishing.

History

1. The Doctrine of Symbolism
2. The Doctrine of Ethos and the Doctrine of Harmonia
3. Benenzon, R. (1981). *Music Therapy Manual* (p. 143). Charles C. Thomas Publishers Limited. Davis, W. B., Gfeller, K. E., & Thaut, M. H. (1992). *An Introduction to Music Therapy: Theory and Practice*. Wm. C. Brown Publisher. Abdel-Salhen, El-Saeed (2005). Music Therapy in Egypt. *Voices Resources*. https://voices.no/ community/index.html?q=country-of-the-month%252F2005-music-therapy-egypt
4. Mereni, A. E. (1996). "Kinesis und kartharsis." The African traditional concept of sound/motion or music: Its application in, and implications for, music therapy. *British Journal of Music Therapy, 10*(1), 17–23.
5. Janzen, J. M. (1992). *Ngoma: Discourses of Healing in Central and Southern Africa*. University of California Press.
6. Wu, Y. (2020). The development of music therapy in Mainland China. *Music Therapy Perspectives, 37*(1), 84–92. Also, Wang, X. (1987). *The Explanation of Shi San Jia. Beijing* (p. 467). Zhonghua Book Company.
7. Sumathy, S. (2005). The ancient healing roots of Indian music. *Voices*. https://voices.no/ community/index.html?q=country%252Fmonthindia_march2005a
8. Sevcik, E. E. (2022). Eva Augusta Vescelius: Life and music career before 1900. *Journal of Music Therapy*. https://doi.org/10.1093/jmt/thac004. Also, Davis, W. B., Gfeller, K. E., & Kahler, E. P. (2018). Music Therapy: A Historical Perspective. In A. J. Knight, A. B. Lagasse, & A. A. Clair (eds), *Music Therapy: An Introduction to the Profession*. American Music Therapy Association.
9. Davis, W. B., Gfeller, K. E., & Kahler, E. P. (2018). Music Therapy: A Historical Perspective. In A. J. Knight, A. B. Lagasse, & A. A. Clair (eds), *Music Therapy: An Introduction to the Profession*. American Music Therapy Association.

Music and Health

1. This paraphrased list of connections over the next few pages can be attributed to Alan P. Merriam, E. Thayer Gaston, William Sears, and Kenneth E. Bruscia, although many writers have provided similar ideas.
2. Patel, A. D. (2008). *Music, Language, and the Brain.* Oxford University Press.
3. Patel, A. D. (2008). *Music, Language, and the Brain.* Oxford University Press. Also Huron, D. & Ollen, J. (2003). Agogic contrast in French and English themes: Further support for Patel and Daniele. *Music Perception, 21,* 267–271.
4. Examples of literature include: Language: Patel, A. D. (2008). *Music, Language, and the Brain.* Oxford University Press. Emotion: Juslin, P. & Sloboda, J. (2011). *Handbook of Music and Emotion.* Oxford University Press. Movement: Ashoori, A., Eagleman, D. M., & Jankovic, J. (2015). Effects of auditory rhythm and music on gait disturbances in Parkinson's Disease. *Frontiers in Neurology, 6,* 234.

Music Therapy Methods

1. These methods are described in Bruscia, K. E. (2014). *Defining Music Therapy.* Barcelona Publishers.

Characteristics of Music

1. Bensimon, M., Amir, D., & Wolf, Y. (2008). Drumming through trauma: Music therapy with post-traumatic soldiers. *The Arts in Psychotherapy, 35,* 34–48. doi:10.1016/j.aip.2007.09.002

Qualities of Musicking

1. Small, C. (1998). *Musicking: The Meanings of Performing and Listening.* Wesleyan University Press.
2. Csikszentmihalyi, M. (1990). *Flow: The Psychology of Optimal Performance.* Harper Perennial. For mention in music therapy, see Das, K. (2011). *The Way of Music: Creating Sound Connections in Music Therapy.* Sarsen Publishing.
3. This table is derived in part from KPAS (Das, 2011; Kalani, 2008; Matney, 2007) with some additions.
4. Kokal, I., Engel, A., Kirschner, S., & Keyserts, C. (2011). Synchronized drumming enhances activity in the caudate and facilitates prosocial commitment – if the rhythm comes easily. *PLoS One, 6,* 11 (November, 2011).
5. Some articles discussing attunement include Trondalen, G. & Skårderud, F. (2007). Playing with affects...and the importance of "affect attunement." *Nordic Journal of Music Therapy, 16,* 100–111, as well as Mossler, K., Schmid, W., Aßmus, J., Fusar-Poll, L., & Gold, C. (2020). Attunement in music therapy for young children with autism: Revisiting qualities of relationship as mechanisms of change. *Journal of Autism and Developmental Disorders, 50*(11), 3921–3934.

The Treatment Process

1. Murakami, B. (2021). The music therapy harm model (MTHM): Conceptualizing harm within music therapy practice. *Revista Científica de Musicoterapia y Disciplinas Afines, 6*(1). https://doi.org/10.24215/27186199e003
2. ibid.
3. ibid.

Therapeutic Music Experiences

1. Bruscia, K. E. (2014). *Defining Music Therapy.* Barcelona Publishers.
2. ibid.
3. Brunk, B. K. (n.d.). *Songwriting for Music Therapists.* Prelude Music Therapy.
4. ibid.
5. ibid.
6. Bruscia, K. E. (2014). *Defining Music Therapy.* Barcelona Publishers. This example shows how receptive and recreative methods mix together.
7. Gardstrom, S. & Hiller, J. (2010). Song discussion as music psychotherapy. *Music Therapy Perspectives, 28,* 147–156.

Theories and Approaches

1. Standley, J., Johnson, C. M., Robb, S. L., Brownell, M. D., & Kim, S. (2008). Behavioral Approach to Music Therapy. In A. Darrow (ed.), *Introduction to Approaches in Music Therapy* (2nd ed., pp.117–119). American Music Therapy Association.
2. ibid.
3. Some traditional developmental theorists from diverse areas include, but are not limited to: Sigmund Freud, Abraham Maslow, Jean Piaget, Urie Bronfenbrenner, Erik Erikson, Lawrence Kohlberg, Arnold Gesell, and Elizabeth Kübler Ross.
4. An example of this approach, which requires extra training, is Helen Bonny's model of Guided Imagery in Music.
5. Voigt, M. (2013). Orff music therapy: History, principles and further development. *Voices, 5*(2), 97–105.
6. Crowe, B. (2004). *Music and Soulmaking.* Scarecrow Press.
7. Schneck, D. J. & Berger, D. (2006). *The Music Effect: Music Physiology and Clinical Applications.* Jessica Kingsley Publishers.
8. Bronfenbrenner, U. (1979). *The Ecology of Human Development: Experiments by Nature and Design.* Harvard University Press.
9. A resource for culturally informed approaches is Stige, B. (2015). *Culture-centered Music Therapy.* Barcelona Publishers. Resources for ecological approaches include Hughes, B. (2004). What happens in music therapy: An ecological approach and theoretical model. *Music Therapy Today, 5*(3), 1–23, and Crooke, A. H. D. (2015). Music therapy, social policy, and ecological models: An example of music in Australian schools. *Voices, 15*(2), n.p.
10. Two primary resources for this orientation are Rolvsjord, R. (2010). *Resource-oriented Music Therapy in Mental Health Care.* Barcelona Publishers, and Rolvsjord, R. (2015). Resource-oriented Perspectives in Music Therapy. In J. Edwards (ed.), *The Oxford Handbook of Music Therapy,* pp. 557–576. Oxford University Press.
11. One can read Bruscia, K. E. (2014). *Defining Music Therapy.* Barcelona Publishers, or

Endnotes

Matney, W. (2019). Music therapy as multiplicity: Implications for music therapy philosophy and theory. *Nordic Journal of Music Therapy, 30,* 3–23. doi: 10.1080/08098131.2020.1811371

Populations and Settings

1.   Dvorak, A. L., Carvalho, S., Rosey, C., Welch, J., *et al.* (2021). *Music Therapy for Adults with Mental Health and Substance Use Conditions.* American Music Therapy Association.
2.   Halverson-Ramos, F., Breyfogle, S., Brinkman, T., Hannan, A., *et al.* (2019). *Music Therapy in Child and Adolescent Behavioral Health.* American Music Therapy Association.
3.   De Witte, M., Pinho, A. D. S., Stams, G., Moonen, X., Bos, A. E. R., & van Hooren, S. (2020). Music therapy for stress reduction: A systematic review and meta-analysis. *Health Psychology Review, 16*(1), 134–159.
4.   Gold, C., Mössler, K., Grocke, D., Heldal, T. O., *et al.* (2013). Individual music therapy for mental health care clients with low therapy motivation: Multicentre randomised controlled trial. *Psychotherapy and Psychosomatics, 82,* 319–331.
5.   Solli, H. P., Rolvsjord, R., & Borg, M. (2013). Toward understanding music therapy as a recovery-oriented practice within mental health care: A meta-synthesis of service users' experiences. *Journal of Music Therapy, 50*(4), 244–273.
6.   McCaffrey, T., Edwards, J., & Fannon, D. (2011). Is there a role for music therapy in the recovery approach in mental health? *The Arts in Psychotherapy, 38,* 135–139.
7.   Hanson-Abromeit, D. & Shaller Gerweck, J. (2010). Obstetrics. In D. Hanson-Abromeit & C. Colwell (eds), *Effective Clinical Practice in Music Therapy: Medical Music Therapy for Adults in Hospital Settings* (pp. 21–96). American Music Therapy Association.
8.   Yinger, O. S. & Gooding, L. F. (2015). A systematic review of music-based interventions for procedural support. *Journal of Music Therapy, 52*(1), 1–77. https://doi.org/10.1093 jmt/thv004
9.   Nelson, K., Adamek, M., & Kleiber, C. (2017). Relaxation training and postoperative music therapy for adolescents undergoing spinal fusion surgery. *Pain Management Nursing: Official Journal of the American Society of Pain Management Nurses, 18*(1), 16–23. https://doi.org/10.1016/j.pmn.2016.10.005
10.   Shaller Gerweck, J. & Tan, X. (2010). Intensive Care Unit (ICU). In D. Hanson-Abromeit & C. Colwell (eds), *Effective Clinical Practice in Music Therapy: Medical Music Therapy for Adults in Hospital Settings* (pp. 97–160). American Music Therapy Association.
11.   Robb, S. L. (2003). *Music Therapy in Pediatric Healthcare: Research and Evidence-based Practice.* American Music Therapy Association.
12.   ibid.
13.   McDougall Miller, D. & O'Callaghan, C. (2010). Cancer Care. In D. Hanson-Abromeit & C. Colwell (eds), *Effective Clinical Practice in Music Therapy: Medical Music Therapy for Adults in Hospital Settings* (pp. 217–283). American Music Therapy Association.
14.   Standley, J. M. & Walworth, D. (2010). *Music Therapy with Premature Infants: Research and Developmental Interventions* (2nd ed.). American Music Therapy Association.
15.   Hanson-Abromeit, D., Shoemark, H., Loewy, J. V., & Colwell, C., (2008). Newborn Intensive Care Unit (NICU). In D. Hanson-Abromeit & C. Colwell (eds), *Effective Clinical Practice in Music Therapy: Medical Music Therapy for Pediatrics in Hospital Settings* (pp. 15–69). American Music Therapy Association.
16.   Loewy, J. (2015). NICU music therapy: Song of kin as critical lullaby in research and practice. *Annals of the New York Academy of Sciences, 1337*(1), 178–185. https:// doi.org/10.1111/nyas.12648
17.   Belgrave, M., Darrow, A.-A., Walworth, D., & Wlodarczyk, N. (2011). *Music Therapy and*

Geriatric Populations: A Handbook for Practicing Music Therapists and Healthcare Professionals. American Music Therapy Association.

18. ibid.

19. ibid.

20. Belgrave, M., Darrow, A.-A., Walworth, D., & Wlodarczyk, N. (2011). In *Music Therapy and Geriatric Populations: A Handbook for Practicing Music Therapists and Healthcare Professionals* (pp. 175–228). American Music Therapy Association.

21. Belgrave, M., Darrow, A.-A., Walworth, D., & Wlodarczyk, N. (2011). In *Music Therapy and Geriatric Populations: A Handbook for Practicing Music Therapists and Healthcare Professionals* (pp. 9–58). American Music Therapy Association.

22. Belgrave, M., Wlodarczyk, N., Walworth, D., & Darrow, A.-A. (2011). *Music Therapy and Geriatric Populations: A Handbook for Practicing Music Therapists and Healthcare Professionals.* American Music Therapy Association.

23. Hilliard, R. E. (2004). A post-hoc analysis of music therapy services for residents in nursing homes receiving hospice care. *Journal of Music Therapy, 41*(4), 266–281. https://doi.org/10.1093/jmt/41.4.266

24. Hilliard, R. E. (2005). Music therapy in hospice and palliative care: A review of the empirical data. *Evidence-Based Complementary and Alternative Medicine, 2*(2), 173–178. https://doi.org/10.1093/ecam/neh076

25. Stige, B., Ansdell, G., Elefant, C., & Pavlicevic, M. (2016). *Where Music Helps: Community Music Therapy in Action and Reflection.* Routledge.

26. Bernard, G. & Dvorak, A. L. (2022). Using music to address trauma with refugees: A systematic review and recommendations. *Music Therapy Perspectives, 41*(1), e30–e43. https://doi.org/10.1093/mtp/miac013.

27. American Music Therapy Association. (2021). *Music Therapy with Military Service Members and Veterans* [Fact Sheet]. www.musictherapy.org/assets/1/7/FactSheet_Music_Therapy_with_Military_Service_Members_and_Veterans_2021.pdf

Resources

1. A useful guide for assessment in general includes Jacobsen, S. L., Waldon, E. G., & Gattino, G. (2018). *Music Therapy Assessment: Theory, Research, and Application.* Jessica Kingsley Publishers.

2. Coleman, K. A. & Brunk, B. K. (1999). *Special Education Music Therapy Process Handbook.* Prelude Music Therapy.

3. Baxter, H. T., Berghofer, J. A., MacEwan, L., Nelson, J., Peters, K., & Roberts, P. (2007). *The Individualized Music Therapy Assessment Profile: IMTAP.* Jessica Kingsley Publishers.

4. Carpente, J. A. (2014). Individual music-centered assessment profile for neurodevelopmental disorders (IMCAP-ND): New developments in music-centered evaluation. *Music Therapy Perspectives, 32*(1), 56–60. And Carpente, J. A. (2013). *Individual Music Centered Assessment Profile for Neurodevelopmental Disorders: A Clinical Manual.* Regina Publishing.

5. Magee, W. L., Siegert, R. J., Daveson, B. A., Lenton-Smith, G., & Taylor, S. M. (2014). Music therapy assessment tool for awareness in disorders of consciousness (MATADOC): Standardisation of the principal subscale to assess awareness in patients with disorders of consciousness. *Neuropsychological Rehabilitation, 24*(1), 101–124.

6. McDermott, O., Orrell, M., & Ridder, H. M. (2015). The development of music in dementia assessment scales (MiDAS). *Nordic Journal of Music Therapy, 24*(3), 232–251. https://doi.org/10.1080/08098131.2014.907333

References

Abdel-Salhen, El-Saeed (2005). Music therapy in Egypt. *Voices Resources*. https://voices.no/community/index.html?q=country-of-the-month%252F2005-music-therapy-egypt

American Music Therapy Association. (2021). *Music Therapy with Military Service Members and Veterans* [Fact Sheet]. www.musictherapy.org/assets/1/7/FactSheet_Music_Therapy_with_Military_Service_Members_and_Veterans_2021.pdf

Ashoori, A., Eagleman, D. M., & Jankovic, J. (2015). Effects of auditory rhythm and music on gait disturbances in Parkinson's Disease. *Frontiers in Neurology, 6,* 234.

Baxter, H. T., Berghofer, J. A., MacEwan, L., Nelson, J., Peters, K., & Roberts, P. (2007). *The Individualized Music Therapy Assessment Profile: IMTAP*. Jessica Kingsley Publishers.

Belgrave, M., Darrow, A.-A., Walworth, D., & Wlodarczyk, N. (2011). *Music Therapy and Geriatric Populations: A Handbook for Practicing Music Therapists and Healthcare Professionals*. American Music Therapy Association.

Benenzon, R. (1981). *Music Therapy Manual* (p. 143). Charles C. Thomas Publishers Limited.

Bensimon, M., Amir, D., & Wolf, Y. (2008). Drumming through trauma: Music therapy with post-traumatic soldiers. *The Arts in Psychotherapy, 35,* 34–48. doi:10.1016/j.aip.2007.09.002

Bernard, G. & Dvorak, A. L. (2022). Using music to address trauma with refugees: A systematic review and recommendations. *Music Therapy Perspectives*, 41(1), e30–e43. https://doi.org/10.1093/mtp/miac013

Bronfenbrenner, U. (1979). *The Ecology of Human Development: Experiments by Nature and Design*. Harvard University Press.

Brunk, B. K. (n.d.). *Songwriting for Music Therapists*. Prelude Music Therapy.

Bruscia, K. E. (2014). *Defining Music Therapy*. Barcelona Publishers.

Carpente, J. A. (2013). *Individual Music Centered Assessment Profile for Neurodevelopmental Disorders: A Clinical Manual*. Regina Publishing.

Carpente, J. A. (2014). Individual music-centered assessment profile for neurodevelopmental disorders (IMCAP-ND): New developments in music-centered evaluation. *Music Therapy Perspectives, 32*(1), 56–60.

Coleman, K. A. & Brunk, B. K. (1999). *Special Education Music Therapy Process Handbook*. Prelude Music Therapy.

Crooke, A. H. D. (2015). Music therapy, social policy, and ecological models: An example of music in Australian schools. *Voices, 15*(2), n.p.

Crowe, B. (2004). *Music and Soulmaking*. Scarecrow Press.

Csikszentmihalyi, M. (1990). *Flow: The Psychology of Optimal Performance*. Harper Perennial.

Das, K. (2011). *The Way of Music: Creating Sound Connections in Music Therapy*. Sarsen Publishing.

Davis, W. B., Gfeller, K. E., & Kahler, E. P. (2018). Music Therapy: A Historical Perspective. In A. J. Knight, A. B. Lagasse, & A. A. Clair (eds), *Music Therapy: An Introduction to the Profession*. American Music Therapy Association..

Davis, W. B., Gfeller, K. E., & Thaut, M. H. (1992). *An Introduction to Music Therapy: Theory and Practice*. Wm. C. Brown Publisher.

De Nora, T. (2000). *Music in Everyday Life*. Cambridge University Press.

De Witte, M., Pinho, A. D. S., Stams, G., Moonen, X., Bos, A. E. R., & van Hooren, S. (2020). Music therapy for stress reduction: A systematic review and meta-analysis. *Health Psychology Review, 16*(1), 134–159.

Dvorak, A. L., Carvalho, S., Rosey, C., Welch, J., *et al.* (2021). *Music Therapy for Adults with Mental Health and Substance Use Conditions.* American Music Therapy Association.

Gardstrom, S. C. & Hiller, J. (2010). Song discussion as music psychotherapy. *Music Therapy Perspectives, 28,* 147–156.

Gold, C., Mössler, K., Grocke, D., Heldal, T. O., *et al.* (2013). Individual music therapy for mental health care clients with low therapy motivation: Multicentre randomised controlled trial. *Psychotherapy and Psychosomatics, 82,* 319–331.

Halverson-Ramos, F., Breyfogle, S., Brinkman, T., Hannan, A., *et al.* (2019). *Music Therapy in Child and Adolescent Behavioral Health.* American Music Therapy Association.

Hanson-Abromeit, D. & Shaller Gerweck, J. (2010). Obstetrics. In D. Hanson-Abromeit & C. Colwell (eds), *Effective Clinical Practice in Music Therapy: Medical Music Therapy for Adults in Hospital Settings* (pp. 21–96). American Music Therapy Association.

Hanson-Abromeit, D., Shoemark, H., Loewy, J. V., & Colwell, C. (2008). Newborn Intensive Care Unit (NICU). In D. Hanson-Abromeit & C. Colwell (eds), *Effective Clinical Practice in Music Therapy: Medical Music Therapy for Pediatrics in Hospital Settings* (pp. 15–69). American Music Therapy Association.

Hilliard, R. E. (2004). A post-hoc analysis of music therapy services for residents in nursing homes receiving hospice care. *Journal of Music Therapy, 41*(4), 266–281. https://doi.org/10.1093/jmt/41.4.266

Hilliard, R. E. (2005). Music therapy in hospice and palliative care: A review of the empirical data. *Evidence-Based Complementary and Alternative Medicine, 2*(2), 173–178. https://doi.org/10.1093/ecam/neh076

Hughes, B. (2004). What happens in music therapy: An ecological approach and theoretical model. *Music Therapy Today, 5*(3), 1–23.

Huron, D. & Ollen, J. (2003). Agogic contrast in French and English themes: Further support for Patel and Daniele. *Music Perception, 21,* 267–271.

Jacobsen, S. L., Waldon, E. G., & Gattino, G. (2018). *Music Therapy Assessment: Theory, Research, and Application.* Jessica Kingsley Publishers.

Janzen, J. M. (1992). *Ngoma: Discourses of Healing in Central and Southern Africa.* University of California Press.

Juslin, P. & Sloboda, J. (2011). *Handbook of Music and Emotion.* Oxford University Press.

Kalani (2008). *All About Hand Percussion.* Alfred Publishing.

Kokal, I., Engel, A., Kirschner, S., & Keyserts, C. (2011). Synchronized drumming enhances activity in the caudate and facilitates prosocial commitment – if the rhythm comes easily. *PLoS One,* 6, 11 (November, 2011).

Loewy, J. (2015). NICU music therapy: Song of kin as critical lullaby in research and practice. *Annals of the New York Academy of Sciences, 1337*(1), 178–185. https://doi.org/10.1111/nyas.12648

Magee, W. L., Siegert, R. J., Daveson, B. A., Lenton-Smith, G., & Taylor, S. M. (2014). Music therapy assessment tool for awareness in disorders of consciousness (MATADOC): Standardisation of the principal subscale to assess awareness in patients with disorders of consciousness. *Neuropsychological Rehabilitation, 24*(1), 101–124.

Matney, B. (2008). *Tataku: The Use of Percussion in Music Therapy.* Sarsen Publishing.

Matney, W. (2019). Music therapy as multiplicity: Implications for music therapy philosophy and theory. *Nordic Journal of Music Therapy, 30,* 3–23. doi: 10.1080/08098131.2020.1811371

References

McCaffrey, T., Edwards, J., & Fannon, D. (2011). Is there a role for music therapy in the recovery approach in mental health? *The Arts in Psychotherapy, 38,* 135–139.

McDermott, O., Orrell, M., & Ridder, H. M. (2015). The development of music in dementia assessment scales (MiDAS). *Nordic Journal of Music Therapy, 24*(3), 232–251. https://doi.org/10.1080/08098131.2014.907333

McDougall Miller, D. & O'Callaghan, C. (2010). Cancer Care. In D. Hanson-Abromeit & C. Colwell (eds), *Effective Clinical Practice in Music Therapy: Medical Music Therapy for Adults in Hospital Settings* (pp. 217–283). American Music Therapy Association.

Mereni, A.E. (1996). "Kinesis und kartharsis." The African traditional concept of sound/motion or music: Its application in, and implications for, music therapy. *British Journal of Music Therapy, 10*(1), 17–23.

Mossler, K., Schmid, W., Aßmus, J., Fusar-Poli, L., & Gold, C. (2020). Attunement in music therapy for young children with autism: Revisiting qualities of relationship as mechanisms of change. *Journal of Autism and Developmental Disorders, 50*(11), 3921–3934.

Murakami, B. (2021). The music therapy harm model (MTHM): Conceptualizing harm within music therapy practice. *Revista Científica de Musicoterapia y Disciplinas Afines, 6*(1). https://doi.org/10.24215/27186199e003

Nelson, K., Adamek, M., & Kleiber, C. (2017). Relaxation training and postoperative music therapy for adolescents undergoing spinal fusion surgery. *Pain Management Nursing: Official Journal of the American Society of Pain Management Nurses, 18*(1), 16–23. https://doi.org/10.1016/j.pmn.2016.10.005

Patel, A. D. (2008). *Music, Language, and the Brain.* Oxford University Press.

Robb, S. L. (2003). *Music Therapy in Pediatric Healthcare: Research and Evidence-Based Practice.* American Music Therapy Association.

Rolvsjord, R. (2010). *Resource-Oriented Music Therapy in Mental Health Care.* Barcelona Publishers.

Rolvsjord, R. (2015). Resource-Oriented Perspectives in Music Therapy. In J. Edwards (ed.), *The Oxford Handbook of Music Therapy* (pp. 557–576). Oxford University Press.

Schneck, D. J. & Berger, D. (2006). *The Music Effect: Music Physiology and Clinical Applications.* Jessica Kingsley Publishers.

Sevcik, E. E. (2022). Eva Augusta Vescelius: Life and music career before 1900. *Journal of Music Therapy.* https://doi.org/10.1093/jmt/thac004

Shaller Gerweck, J. & Tan, X. (2010). Intensive Care Unit (ICU). In D. Hanson-Abromeit & C. Colwell (eds), *Effective Clinical Practice in Music Therapy: Medical Music Therapy for Adults in Hospital Settings* (pp. 97–160). American Music Therapy Association.

Small, C. (1998). *Musicking: The Meanings of Performing and Listening.* Wesleyan University Press.

Solli, H. P., Rolvsjord, R., & Borg, M. (2013). Toward understanding music therapy as a recovery-oriented practice within mental health care: A meta-synthesis of service users' experiences. *Journal of Music Therapy, 50*(4), 244–273.

Standley, J., Johnson, C. M., Robb, S. L., Brownell, M. D., & Kim, S. (2008). Behavioral Approach to Music Therapy. In A. Darrow (ed.), *Introduction to Approaches in Music Therapy* (2nd ed., pp. 117–119). American Music Therapy Association.

Standley, J. M. & Walworth, D. (2010). *Music Therapy with Premature Infants: Research and Developmental Interventions* (2nd ed.). American Music Therapy Association.

Stige, B. (2015). *Culture-Centered Music Therapy.* Barcelona Publishers.

Stige, B., Ansdell, G., Elefant, C., & Pavlicevic, M. (2016). *Where Music Helps: Community Music Therapy in Action and Reflection.* Routledge.

Sumathy, S. (2005). The ancient healing roots of Indian music. *Voices.* https://voices.no/community/index.html?q=country%252Fmonthindia_march2005a

Trondalen, G. & Skårderud, F. (2007). Playing with affects...and the importance of "affect attunement." *Nordic Journal of Music Therapy, 16,* 100–111.

Voigt, M. (2013). Orff music therapy: History, principles and further development. *Voices, 5*(2), 97–105.

Wang, X. (1987). *The Explanation of Shi San Jia. Beijing* (p. 467). Zhonghua Book Company.

Wikimedia Foundation. (2023, January 6). *Writing about music is like dancing about architecture.* Wikipedia. https://en.wikipedia.org/wiki/Writing_about_music_is_like_dancing_about_architecture

Wu, Y. (2020). The development of music therapy in Mainland China. *Music Therapy Perspectives, 37*(1), 84–92.

Yinger, O. S. & Gooding, L. F. (2015). A systematic review of music-based interventions for procedural support. *Journal of Music Therapy, 52*(1), 1–77. https://doi.org/10.1093/jmt/thv004

Index